T0158811

A Path to
Restoration

A Study Guide

Lois Brittell, PhD

WESTBOW
P R E S S®
A DIVISION OF THOMAS NELSON
& ZONDERVAN

Copyright © 2016 Lois Brittell, PhD.

All rights reserved. No part of this book may be used or reproduced by any means, graphic, electronic, or mechanical, including photocopying, recording, taping or by any information storage retrieval system without the written permission of the author except in the case of brief quotations embodied in critical articles and reviews.

This book is a work of non-fiction. Unless otherwise noted, the author and the publisher make no explicit guarantees as to the accuracy of the information contained in this book and in some cases, names of people and places have been altered to protect their privacy.

Scripture quotations are from The Holy Bible, English Standard Version® (ESV®), copyright © 2001 by Crossway, a publishing ministry of Good News Publishers. Used by permission. All rights reserved.

Scripture taken from the Amplified Bible, copyright © 1954, 1958, 1962, 1964, 1965, 1987 by The Lockman Foundation. Used by permission.

WestBow Press books may be ordered through booksellers or by contacting:

WestBow Press
A Division of Thomas Nelson & Zondervan
1663 Liberty Drive
Bloomington, IN 47403
www.westbowpress.com
1 (866) 928-1240

Because of the dynamic nature of the Internet, any web addresses or links contained in this book may have changed since publication and may no longer be valid. The views expressed in this work are solely those of the author and do not necessarily reflect the views of the publisher, and the publisher hereby disclaims any responsibility for them.

Any people depicted in stock imagery provided by Thinkstock are models, and such images are being used for illustrative purposes only. Certain stock imagery © Thinkstock.

ISBN: 978-1-5127-4992-2 (sc)
ISBN: 978-1-5127-4993-9 (hc)
ISBN: 978-1-5127-4991-5 (e)

Library of Congress Control Number: 2016911592

Print information available on the last page.

WestBow Press rev. date: 8/16/2016

Dedicated

To those who are seeking restoration

CONTENTS

FOREWORD

So, so thankful for *It's All about Him* …

Why? A pastor, as a shepherd, wants the best for his or her flock. We are keenly aware that we ourselves are simply sheep who are shepherding other sheep under the guidance of the True Shepherd, the Good Shepherd, the Lord Jesus Christ.

In pastoral care, we know that from time to time, one needs not only a pastor and the support of other Christians but also a professional therapist. I, like most pastors, do not suggest that the person simply gets therapy; nor do we suggest a therapist at random. Rather, we seek to entrust those in our flock to a godly, professional therapist.

Pastors, in seeking a therapist, often rely upon recommendations from other pastors. Still, we want to know if we can trust that therapist with our own flock. Many of us will first meet with a therapist to determine whether we feel comfortable with recommending him or her.

When I first meet with therapists, I ask them about their practice with relation to their faith. As licensed psychologist, Dr. Lois Brittell truthfully reveals *It's All about Him*. First of all, I am seeking a Christian therapist—not only a therapist who happens to be a believer in Jesus Christ but a therapist whose faith truly informs his or her practice. You are welcome to read that again: I am seeking a therapist whose faith truly informs his or her practice.

"What does that look like?" I ask the potential therapist. "Walk me through a session you might have with a person, a fellow believer, whom I, as a pastor, would refer to you. That is, tell me how you would have both your faith and your professional training as a therapist come together to counsel a believer."

Can you imagine how excited I was to read Dr. Brittell's new book *A Path to Restoration: A Study Guide?* Such an amazing guide for the therapist who is a Christian and seeks to be faithful in the practice of therapy! This book is not only for the therapist but also for the student, the pastor, the believer who seeks intimacy with God, and for the one who wonders about God and how He might intersect with one's own life at the deepest levels.

Excitedly, I strongly requested Dr. Brittell to write a study guide to accompany *It's All about Him.* Little did I know that she would write that, but so much more! The book you hold now in your hands could easily have begun with the same words as in Dr. Luke's book of Acts. "In my former book, Theophilus, I wrote about … Jesus."

Dear Theophilus—that is, dear lover of God—are you one who loves God? Do you seek to serve Him in all you do? Then this book is for you. And truly, *It's All about Him.*

Peace,
Reverend E. Wayne Kempton, Minister of Pastoral Care
Community Presbyterian Church, Ventura, California

GRATITUDE

My greatest gratitude is to God! He chose me, redeemed me, and restored my soul.

When I was deeply distressed, God brought me to the church of his choosing where the restoration of my soul began. My gratitude to Pastor Kent Meads for his pastoral care, sermons, mentoring, and friendship is a lifelong gratitude. God does the restoration, but he has always worked through people, including the Christ. God chose Pastor Kent to provide what was essential for my restoration. He listened to my pain; never passed judgment—just listened and provided godly wisdom, always drawing my attention to Jesus. His ministry and friendship have had a major impact on my life as well as on the formation of this book. For his presence in my life, I am deeply grateful.

Pastor Wayne Kempton served as the first reader, advisor, and editor for content. His guidance in editing and clarifying my thoughts, as well as my theology, has been invaluable. His enthusiastic response to the publication of the original book was a source of continual encouragement for writing this one. For his prayers, the many hours of editing, and his support, I am extremely grateful.

To Sharon Wilgenburg, the copy editor, who provided the knowledge and expertise for all things technical and mechanical, I am very grateful. I praise God that he did not call me to that specialty. I am equally grateful he called her to it.

The gifts of friendship and support from the Newells and the Zimmermans continue to be a cause for praise. For my friend and support person, Sonja Morgan, I am very grateful. Friendship is a profound gift from the hand of God.

To the many patients who entrusted me with a portion of their lives, I am grateful for your part in my life and for the healing God granted you.

For the many friends and family members who have been part of my life and from whom I learned more about God, I thank him.

I continue to praise God for my housekeeper, Yolanda Robledo.

To the editors at Westbow Press I am grateful for their encouragement and insight.

For God's extravagant love for us, and for me, my gratitude is eternal.

Blessings

PREFACE

In the original book, *It's All about Him: Intimacy with God*, I asked "Why another book?" For this one, I know the answer to that question. The original book was, by design, densely packed with Scripture. The book is so densely filled with Scripture that some readers have used it as a devotional book. At the time of its writing, I had no idea I would write a study guide. However, as the comments came in from *It's All about Him*, I realized readers wanted to be able to make notes as they studied the references. Therefore, a study guide seemed desirable and necessary.

Additionally, I wanted to emphasize specific topics. The study guide has given me the opportunity to highlight these issues and to present the chapters in parts that are related to one another. Grouping topics of similar emphasis has been helpful to me as the writer; I believe it will give greater clarity and understanding to the reader.

The study guide will give readers greater opportunity to develop intimacy with God. Once you have been born again, the desire to be more intimate with God is, I hope, a lifelong desire on the part of every reader. Nothing can replace the joy of knowing and relating to God in ever-increasing intimacy.

While it is a study guide for the reader, the second half of the book is, at the same time, a partial account of my own journey from almost complete detachment and emotional numbness into intimacy with God. His grace, mercy, and guidance are obvious in every chapter. His ability and desire for restoration are not unique to me. The Bible is full of stories of restoration, several of them recounted in the study guide. To be redeemed, having lost my way as a result of disobedience, and then to be restored still feels like a miracle in which I rejoice every day.

God offers amazing grace to all his children. If you have not been bought back from Satan's influence, let me encourage you to seek God's face today. Those who seek him will find him. Then, if you have wandered into the weeds following redemption, let me encourage you to pray for forgiveness and restoration. If you need help, seek counsel from a godly pastor or godly professional. His grace is always sufficient.

INTRODUCTION

The following study guide was written at the request of several of those who read the original book. Pastor Wayne Kempton expressed his desire for it to be written to help those who read it gain a deeper understanding of what it means to have intimacy with God.

My daughter wanted to be able to make notes as she went along. Making notes can help imprint a topic more effectively. I wanted to expand on some of the topics, and I felt the Lord urging me to write it.

The organization of the topics will follow the plan of the original book. In addition to the chapters, there are four parts. The first part looks at "What He Has Done." The title of the first chapter, "It's All about Him," sets the tone. Then it asks, "Who is he?" This chapter leaves one with a sense of the "hugeness" of God. The Creator and Sustainer of the universe, for whom, by whom, and through whom all things have been created, is obviously larger than natural life. The focus is on the almightiness of God.

Chapter 2, "Created by Him," asks, "Why was I born?" The question is answered in recognizing that Adam and Eve, the first human beings, were created in the image of God to reflect his glory. It didn't take long for them to choose to follow Satan's beguilement rather than to be obedient to God. The image of God in Adam and Eve was marred as a result, and the man and his wife were punished and separated from God by being thrown out of the garden. The plan to redeem humanity was predicted in the curse put upon Satan.

The fruit of the Spirit is introduced in this chapter.

In chapter 3, "Identity in Him," we explore, "Who am I?" What is my identity? Our identity is made up of various aspects of our God-given gifts, including how we look, our gifts and talents, how we use our God-given gifts, and the fact that Christ has purchased us. We are no longer obligated to obey Satan. God has chosen us to be adopted into his family. We are temples of the Holy Spirit who has been given us as a seal of our salvation. The Holy Spirit helps us live a godly life. Recognizing the voice of the Holy Spirit is essential to living a life of obedience. The gifts of the Spirit are presented.

The next part focuses on "What He Asks of Us."

In chapter 4, "Loving Him," we ask, "What is the greatest commandment?" The answer is "You shall love the Lord your God with all your heart and with all your soul and with all your mind and with all your strength" (Mark 12:30). We are commanded to love him with our entire being. He says we "shall." That "shall" is an imperative; it is not optional. He says our entire being is to be active in loving God. When we review the preceding chapters and acknowledge how "huge," how full of love, and how faithful God is, it makes sense that our entire being is to be involved in loving him. We find the biblical definition of love in 1 Corinthians 13:4–8.

Chapter 5, "Love Your Neighbor as Yourself: In Him," says we are to love our neighbor as ourselves. I ask, "Who is my neighbor?" Anyone but God can be our neighbor. This chapter presents several relationships on the human level. Marriages and friendships are used as examples of love for one another. Together with the preceding commandment this commandment makes up the greatest commandment, as stated by Christ. Since God is love, it makes sense that the greatest commandment would be about love. His love for us is everlasting. We are to reflect his defining attribute of love in our interactions with others.

In chapter 6, I ask, "How Can I Have Intimacy with God?"

"Praying to Him: Intimacy with God" focuses on prayer as the expression of intimacy with God. Prayer is communication with God. It is logical that we would, or should, want to talk with the most important person in the universe: our Creator, Lover, and God. Examples of prayers of confession, praise, and oneness are given. The Lord's Prayer is given as an example of a simple prayer that is easy to learn for anyone beginning to develop a prayer life. Communication is a two-way activity. Therefore, learning to listen to and wait on God is part of an active prayer life. He says to pray without ceasing.

The second half of the book presents the more psychological aspect of the book. The third part of the study guide is titled "What Sometimes Happens." The verse that expresses this most clearly says, "All we like sheep have gone astray."

Chapter 7, "Anxiety, or Peace with Him," specifically addresses anxiety: how it is defined, how it feels, what can cause it, and why God says not to have it. The question is "Can I be free from anxiety?" A portion of this chapter clarifies how biblical truth can address the primary cause of anxiety; insecurity, or fear of insecurity. Some personal history is given.

Chapter 8, "Depression, or Contentment with Him," is about depression. The question is "How can I be content?" Earlier definitions of depression included anger turned inward and frozen rage. When managed care came to the forefront, the causal definition changed to having something chemically wrong with the brain. While a percentage of depression is organically determined, depression is seen primarily as a mood disorder. Antidepressants change the mood but do little to explore the causes of the pain from loss and the anger that are most often at the root of depression. It is essential to explore that loss. Biblical ways of dealing with loss and anger are presented.

In chapter 9, "Arrogance, or Humility before Him," the command to humble oneself is presented as an imperative. "How can I humble myself?" Arrogance and pride, instead of humility, are often our choice when we go astray. Jesus is presented as the model of humility, based on Philippians 2. The evil that comes into the world as a result of arrogance began with Satan and continues to this day. Humility is neither a gift nor a fruit of the Spirit. It is a choice. We are commanded to obey. The rewards of humility are presented.

The last part of the book is titled "Restoration in Him." The reference is Romans 8:28. In chapter 10, "Detachment, or Trust in Him," the question is "Would I ever be able to feel again?" This part is based largely on my personal experience, both painful and restorative. Chapter 10 demonstrates how I began to lose my trust in God. Rather than running toward him, I chose the defense mechanism of detachment. Eventually, I became almost totally emotionally numb; I felt unable to find him.

What amazed me was that I was able to be effective while practicing in my office, teaching, or speaking at engagements, even while I was numb in my personal life. A certain amount of detachment is helpful in treating people. You don't want to internalize their pain, so even in the detachment God was empowering me.

In chapter 11, "Conviction, Consequences, Condemnation, or Grace from Him," I wrestled with whether God was convicting me or whether I was reaping consequences. The question is "Am I being given grace or being convicted—having consequences or being condemned?" The passages regarding reaping had always been presented to me as a threat for misbehavior. Within the context of the passage, it is clear the Lord is speaking of reaping in terms of rewards. Then I realized he was both convicting and providing consequences. Much of the pain had come into my life because I had married an unbeliever. (He later became a believer.) I feel the teaching of consequences has been sorely missed in our culture. Consequences are the natural outcome of whatever behavior one has engaged in. We seem to understand this more readily in the natural world than in the spiritual or psychological world. Both are equally true. I understood that I was being given grace and not being condemned because God had chosen me.

Chapter 12, "Restoration by Him," is the culmination of my life story up to this point. The statement is "I have been restored!" My soul has been restored. God has restored my soul. When I think of David, who wrote those words, I see that those who love deeply are capable of great sin. While I was writing this chapter, I came to understand the sovereignty of God with greater clarity. Nothing escapes God's notice or falls outside his love. In learning to trust in his sovereignty, I have found the place of quietness and rest that he promised. He has restored my soul.

To God be the glory

Part 1

WHAT HE HAS DONE

And God saw everything that he had made, and behold, it was very good.
—Genesis 1:31

1

It's All about Him

**Who is He? Who is God?
I wanted to know.**

Yours, O Lord, is the greatness and the power and the glory and
the victory and the majesty, for all that is in the heavens and in
the earth is yours. Yours is the kingdom, O Lord, and you are
exalted as head above all. Both riches and honor come from you,
and you rule over all. In your hand are power and might, and
in your hand it is to make great and to give strength to all. And
now we thank you, our God, and praise your glorious name.
—1 Chronicles 29:11–13

Toward a Better Understanding of God's Greatness

This chapter is designed to help you know more about God—about
who he is and about how to know him more intimately. David, the author
of the above passage, knew God's greatness personally when he wrote these
words. The Lord had taken him from tending his father's sheep to being
king of Israel. As a shepherd, David had killed lions and bears that were
attempting to attack the sheep. After having been anointed king of Israel,
he was pursued by the former king, Saul, who attempted to kill him on

several occasions. David understood that his strength and wisdom came from God. God thought so highly of him that he chose David to be in Christ's lineage. Jesus is referred to as the Son of David (Matthew 1:1). Luke 1:32 says Christ will sit on the throne of his father, David. God and David enjoyed deep intimacy.

Intimacy is defined as "belonging to or characterizing one's deepest nature: being marked by close association, contact or familiarity: marked by a warm friendship developing through long association."[1] According to that definition, deep friendship developed between God and David. A close association emerged from their deepest natures. This is borne out in the statement that David was "a man after God's own heart" (1 Samuel 13:14). What an incredible honor.

One of the most significant accounts of the intimacy between God and David occurs when the Lord tells David that he, God, will build a house for David (2 Samuel 7). Usually people build a house for God or their gods. However, in this case God, Jehovah, is going to build a house for David, a human—a remarkable situation suggesting a very special relationship between God and David. David was overwhelmed by this gift. The account is well worth reading.

When you read the psalms, you find that David adored God. He prayed to him, meditated on him, loved him, and waited on him. In 2 Samuel, David asked God's permission about going to war on several occasions. God and David enjoyed mutual love and respect. In a later chapter, we will look more closely at David's activity with God. Intimacy requires interaction and communication. Clearly, both were evident between God and David.

The Lord forgave David when he repented for having committed adultery and murder (Psalm 51). However, the Lord did not grant David's request when he asked that his son, conceived in adultery, might be healed. The boy died: had he lived, the Lord would have been rewarding sin.

David lived on the raw edges of life. Yet God exalted him for his humility. Their story is a profound example of intimacy between a man and his God and between God and his man.

Do you want an intimate relationship with the living God?

---

[1]   *Merriam-Webster's Collegiate Dictionary*, 11th ed., s.v. "intimacy."

If not, this may not be the book for you. If you are unsure, try doing some of the exercises to see if learning more about God might be fun and rewarding. It can't hurt.

How Can You Learn to Know God Intimately?

If you want an intimate relationship with God, let's begin by seeking to understand the words David used in the passage at the beginning of the chapter according to their true definitions. He uses words that you don't use in your everyday conversation. Begin by looking up their definitions in the dictionary. As I was writing this, I realized I didn't feel comfortable with my understanding of the word *majesty*. It is not a word I use often. It means splendor. That is a word I feel more comfortable with. Perhaps some of the following words will become more comfortable as you look them up in the dictionary and record their meanings:

- greatness

- power

- glory

- victory

- majesty

For example, *great* means "notably large in size: HUGE." Other definitions include "remarkable in effectiveness … preeminent … markedly superior."[2] This is how the dictionary defines the word great.

Have you ever thought of God as being huge?

What does it mean to you to think of God as being huge?

How is your current perception different from your previous understanding of God?

Find scriptures to fill in the meanings by using a concordance. God's greatness will become more evident as you reflect on these passages.

For example, Deuteronomy 3:24–25 is a wonderful passage of praise spoken by Moses. It speaks of God's greatness and shows the intimacy that existed between God and Moses. Moses said,

> "O Lord God, you have only begun to show your servant your
> greatness and your mighty hand. For what god is there in heaven
> or on earth who can do such works and mighty acts as yours?"

Moses said this just after the Lord told him he could not enter the Promised Land. He was barred because he had hit the rock rather than speaking to it, to bring forth water for the endlessly complaining Israelites (Deuteronomy 1:37). Still, intimacy is clearly evident. Moses boldly asked to be allowed to go in. Although the Lord refused Moses's request, the subsequent verses show that the trust between them was not broken. God declared that he spoke to Moses face-to-face as a man speaks to his friend (Exodus 33:11). Friendship can be intimate.

---

[2]   *Merriam-Webster's Collegiate Dictionary*, 11th ed., s.v. "great."

Take a minute to reflect on the relationship between God and Moses.

How does God speak to you as to a friend? Do you want him to?

Following this format will help you gain an in-depth understanding of a great deal of scripture. Be sure to read several verses before and after the references you have chosen in the concordance. Knowing the context will give you a better understanding of what God is doing in the passage. Doing this kind of study with any word in the Bible about which you are curious can be fun and enlightening. I have done word studies on clothes, wine, anxiety, war, and many other words about which I had a desire to know what God said.

Look up the next descriptor of God in the dictionary.

Power: "The ability to act or produce an effect ... official authority, capacity or right."[3]

Next, look up several references in the concordance for the word power.

The concordance I used had three columns of references. Not all the verses apply to what you want to understand about God. However, many of them do. Psalm 71:18–21 is a good passage to internalize if you are in the second half of life.

> So even to old age and gray hairs, O God, do not forsake me until I proclaim your might to another generation, your power to all those to come. Your righteousness, O God, reaches the high heavens. You who have done great things, O God, who is like you? You who have made me see many troubles and calamities will revive me again: from the depths of the earth you will bring me up again. You will increase my greatness, and comfort me again.

What a beautiful expression of intimacy.

---

[3]   *Merriam-Webster's Collegiate Dictionary*, 11th ed., s.v. "power."

Intimacy with God will depend largely on how much time you put into prayer and into internalizing scripture. "I have stored up your word in my heart, that I might not sin against you" (Psalm 119:11). Internalizing scripture and choosing obedience and intimacy with God rather than sinning always brings joy. And you always have a choice! Intimacy with the living God is always the most rewarding and fulfilling way to live.

Follow this format for all five major words used to describe God in 1 Chronicles 29. It will give you a much better perspective of how God describes himself.

Other References Regarding God's Greatness

The earth is the Lord's and the fullness thereof, the world and those who dwell therein.
—Psalm 24:1

Thus says the Lord, who created the heavens and stretched them out, who spread out the earth and what comes from it, who gives breath to the people on it and spirit to those who walk in it: "I am the Lord; I have called you in righteousness; *I will take you by the hand and keep you.*"
—Isaiah 42:5–6 (emphasis added)

What does this tell you about God? What do you feel?

In what way is he more powerful than you thought?

This great, powerful God who created the entire universe is holding your hand and knows the number of hairs on your head (Matthew 10:31).

He knows your thoughts before you speak them (Psalm 139:4). He gives you breath and spirit. He holds the breath of all humankind in his hand (Job 12:10). Pretty awesome, isn't he? God is giving you breath as well as life and all good things.

"All things were made through him, and without him was not anything made that was made" (John 1:3; emphasis added). He made the eye of the housefly. He made the materials that make up the MRI equipment, and he gave humanity the wisdom to put it all together to make a wondrous machine that can reveal the inside of the human body

> The God who made the world and everything in it, being Lord of heaven and earth … gives to all mankind life and breath and everything … *Yet he is actually not far from each one of us, for in him we live and move and have our being.*
> —Acts 17:24, 25, 27, 28 (emphasis added)

> *For by him all things were created,* in heaven and on earth, visible and invisible, whether thrones or dominions or rulers or authorities—all things *were created through him and for him. And he is before all things, and in him all things hold together.*
> —Colossians 1:16–17 (emphasis added)

What are your reactions to the fact that the Creator of the universe is holding your hand, and also sustaining the whole of creation?

Do you feel overwhelmed? If you do, linger there a while.

God Is Active in Our Lives

His creativity is limitless. Not only did he create the universe, he also created the elements that man has used to fashion amazing things since the time of creation.

Have you praised him?

David wrote many praises, some of which you might want to internalize. *To praise* means "to glorify (a god or saint) esp. by the attribution of perfections."[4] In your concordance, you will find many references to praise in the psalms. Praise is something that God desires. You know how much you like to receive a compliment. Well, you were made in his image to reflect him and to be like him (Genesis 1:27). If you like compliments, you can understand how much he wants praise, given how much greater he is and how much greater his works are than you and your works. The passages previously quoted from Acts 17 and Colossians 1 also give you cause for praise. If you would like to write some of your own praises in this book, it is for your use and your creativity. Be as creative as you want. He has given you all good things.

---

[4]   *Merriam-Webster's Collegiate Dictionary,* 11th ed., s.v. "praise."

The "Allness" of God

He created all light.
He created all darkness.
He created all life.
He created all death.
He created all height.
He created all depth.
He created all width.
He created all length.
He created all galaxies.
He created all grains of sand.
He created all oceans.
He created all deserts.
He created the color spectrum.
He created the sound waves.
He created all angels.
He created all earthworms.
He created all hearts.
He created all minds.
He created you.
He created me.
He created all friendships.
Thank you, God!

What are your "allnesses"? Add them to the above poem.

Who are the special people in your life?

Why are they special to you?

What are your favorite things?

What makes them special?

What are your favorite ideas?

What do you especially appreciate about them?

What do you like most about God?

Can you explain?

In writing the poem, I struggled, wondering if it were true. Did God really create all things? I asked my mentor if it were true. He pondered it for a while, then said yes, it is true. For example, my driveway has earthworms that have crawled up there seeking to escape the sprinklers. Did God really create them? Then I remembered that the word *genesis* means "the beginning." God made the beginnings of all things.

The verses quoted earlier in the chapter state that God made the world and everything in it. Ecclesiastes 11:5 says, "As you do not know the way the spirit comes to the bones in the womb of a woman with child, *so you do not know the work of God who makes everything*" (emphasis added). One of my pastors had looked up the word *everything* in the Greek and it meant "every thing." As you read the Bible, ponder what it says and how it relates to your life experiences. God knows the number of each hair on the head of each one of us (Matthew 10:30). Everything means everything.

Learn to praise God for every good and perfect gift in your life.

Two more gifts that God provides are riches and honor (1 Chronicles 29:12). They often go together. If you have riches, you will probably receive honor as well. Several of the Proverbs mention how riches draw friends and poverty often leaves a person friendless. David had certainly been given both riches and friends. Even in today's cultures, the wealthy are often given honor above others.

Do you want riches and honor? They come from God. Ask him to provide them. He may ask something of you in return.

In the current social climate, there are so many ways to attempt to grasp riches and honor. The political scene is rife with illegitimate ways to obtain them. First Chronicles 29 says riches and honor come from God. Since he is sovereign and holds the breath of all mankind in his hand, it seems logical that he is able to dispense riches and honor according to his divine will. I wondered how so many people have gotten wealth or honor through illegitimate means and how they seem to be getting away with it.

Then I read Psalms 37 and 73. Psalm 37 begins, "Fret not yourself because of evildoers … for they will soon fade like the grass and wither like the green herb." It speaks of the contrast between those who trust God to give them wealth and honor, those who get wealth and honor through evil means, and the different outcomes for each of them. Psalm 73:17 says, "But when I thought how to understand this, it seemed to me a wearisome task, until I went into the sanctuary of God; then I discerned their end." While the temptation to grasp riches and honor can be great, God is not lax concerning his promises. He will provide consequences for both categories of people according to their works. Read chapters 37 and 73 in their entirety. You will find so much reassurance there.

How do you plan to obtain wealth, honor, or both?

What would you do with them if you obtained them?

Some of God's Other Unique Qualities

There are no surprises with God. In addition to being endlessly creative, he is omniscient—all-knowing. *He knows every day of the rest of your life.* God has always known all things from before time, as we know it, to eternity. Eternity never ends: it is forever. The finite mind cannot wholly understand this. In fact, for some it is downright scary. I don't claim to understand it. However, he said it, so I attempt to believe it as an act of faith.

The psalms contain several verses stating that God, in his all-knowingness, knows our thoughts even before we express them.

> O Lord, you have searched me and known me! You know when I sit down and when I rise up; you discern my thoughts from afar. You search out my path and my lying down and are acquainted with all my ways. Even before a word is on my tongue, behold, O Lord, you know it altogether.
>
> —Psalm 139:1–4

Some people get confused about God's foreknowledge; they think that since he has foreknowledge, they have no free will. Does knowing that your child will take a cookie as soon as your back is turned remove choice for him? Obviously not. Neither does God's foreknowledge remove our choices. In John 6, Jesus is teaching a large group of disciples or followers. The teaching was that they should eat his flesh and drink his blood. Even though he explained that it was a spiritual eating and drinking, many were offended by the teaching. "Jesus knew from the beginning who those were who did not believe, and who it was who would betray him" (John 6:64).

They were free to exercise their will: they had the freedom to choose. He just knew how they would choose.

After this, he asked his twelve disciples if they, too, wanted to stop following him.

Peter said, "Lord, to whom shall we go? You have the words of eternal life" (John 6:68). That is just as true today as when Peter said it.

Have you tried to go elsewhere for the answers to life's questions?

How did that work out for you?

Record your thoughts about his omniscience.

The Lord knew who would be on the planes of September 11, 2001. He knew who would fly into heaven and who would not. He is such an amazing God. As humans, we not only fall short of the glory of God (Romans 3:23), but we often fail to understand the enormity of his being. Throughout the Bible, he has warned us about what to expect if we choose not to obey or honor him as God. He delights when you recognize him for who He is and what he has done. He loves praise and worship. You are made in his image. You, too, want to be recognized. You love compliments.

Sometimes he gives you something I call "love notes from God." They can be a surprise email, a compliment from someone who doesn't usually give compliments, an unexpected bit of tenderness, or wearing the same colors as your friend without having talked about it beforehand. They are reminders that he is watching over you and holding you by the hand and that he will never leave you or forsake you.

This is such an enormous promise. How does it feel to you?

Your choices will always have consequences, either godly or painful. Look up and record some of the passages that deal with consequences for honoring, or not honoring, God as God. Proverbs 16:5–9 gives a short example.

God is also omnipotent; that means he is all-powerful. Having created the universe by the power of his word and having raised Jesus by his power, you might ask if there is anything too hard (marvelous) for God, knowing that the answer is no. His power, evident in creation, may be hard for us to understand. For pure delight and enjoyment, read Job 38 through 41. The Lord asks Job some really significant questions. God speaks of having created the world, the things that are in it, and the things that occur in it. Set aside some time to meditate on the verses and picture what he says.

Someday, all people will be raised from the dead, some to be with him forever, some to be apart from him forever. Let yourself think about the amount of power it takes to raise someone from the dead. It reminds me of the book of Genesis when God created the universe by the power of his word; he spoke it into existence: unlimited power.

How can a person understand that kind of power?

What are your thoughts? Do you think there is anything too hard for God?

If so, what do you think it would be?

God is also omnipresent, always present with each one. You are never alone. When you are part of his family, you have the security of knowing he is always with you and in you through the presence of the Holy Spirit. The Spirit has been given to you for several reasons: to keep you from feeling like an orphan (John 14:18), to convict you of sin and righteousness and judgment (John 16:8–11), and as a seal or guarantee that you belong to God (2 Corinthians 1:22). A delightful little book, *The Practice of the Presence of God* (Lawrence, 1982), gives simple suggestions on how to learn to practice God's presence in even the humblest circumstances. To the degree that I have learned to practice his presence, I have found a sense of security, safety, and God's love. Practicing his presence requires frequent communication, as is necessary in any good relationship.

How do you practice being aware of his presence?

Loneliness is one of the greatest cultural problems of our time. The more time you spend with your electronic gadgets, including TV, the lonelier you become. Some additional causes of loneliness are broken families, abandoned children, and alcohol-or drug-abusing parents. God knew before the creation of the world that loneliness would be a major problem. He knew that sin separates us from him, from each other, and from our internal selves. He offers you the opportunity to become part of his family and offers intimacy with himself as the solution to loneliness.

The more you practice intimacy with God, the more you will come to cherish his presence. The Creator and Sustainer of the universe will never leave you or forsake you. If you stay within his will, you will experience his presence in all things, even the tough things. With God, never leaving you means never leaving you.

What reassurance do you find in the Bible? Look up several of the verses that say God will never leave you or forsake you. Record some of your favorites so you can find them quickly when Satan tries to make you feel angry, depressed, or sad while feeling that you are lost or alone.

God says he chose you to be in Christ before the foundation of the world (Ephesians 1:4). Before the foundation of the world is a very significant time frame. It means before time as we know it began. Is it logical, then, that he would forget or leave you?

How do you feel when you think of how intimately God knows you (Psalm 139)? He knows your thoughts before you do. Remember he has numbered the hairs on your head (Matthew 10:30). Try to put your thoughts and feelings into words.

Since he chose you, do you have any say in controlling your life? Do you have free will and choice? Many passages in the Bible refer to the significance of choice. One of the most specific is below.

> I call heaven and earth to witness against you today, that I have set before you life and death, blessing and curse. *Therefore choose life* that you and your offspring may live, loving the Lord your God, obeying his voice and holding fast to him.
> —Deuteronomy 30:19–20 (emphasis added)

That is a clear statement about choice.

Further chapters following that injunction in Deuteronomy reveal God's heart for his children (Deuteronomy 31–34). They are well worth reading.

> For you are a people holy to the Lord your God. The Lord your God has chosen you to be a people for his treasured possession, out of all the peoples who are on the face of the earth. It was not because you were more in number than any other people that the Lord set his love on you and chose you, for you were the fewest of all peoples, but it is because the Lord loves you and is keeping the oath that he swore to your fathers, that the Lord has brought you out with a mighty hand and redeemed you.
> —Deuteronomy 7:6–8

How do you react to what you have just read?

Theologians have debated for centuries whether it is God's choice or our choice that makes the difference in becoming part of his family. Many passages in the New Testament refer to the *elect*, which means God's choice. In the Old Testament, Israel was clearly defined as God's chosen people. Look up some of the passages in your concordance that relate to the elect. You will find several in the book of Acts. Romans 8:29–30 speaks of your having been predestined to become a child of God, part of his family. In the Old Testament, God often reminds the nation of Israel that he chose them to be his special people. The argument against this position is that it seems exclusionary. Perhaps it does. However, it is God's Word and his choice.

A different school of thought suggests that your choice is the overriding principle in determining whether you become part of God's family or not. The primary idea supporting this position is the verse that says, "Whoever will" or "Whosoever will" (John 3:16:). "For God so loved the world, that he gave his only son, that whoever believes in him should not perish but have eternal life."

As you look at this verse, you see that God loved the world. God is the initiator. The Lord is very clear that it is his will to give his children all good things, including eternal life. You can't even breathe unless he gives you breath. The argument against this position is that it puts man in charge of the universe and salvation and leaves God as a necessary accessory. Be careful to refrain from assuming that your wishing motivates God the Father to choose you. God is always the initiator.

Joshua, who led the children of Israel following Moses's death, challenged the Israelites to choose God (Joshua 22:5, 23:6, 24:14–15, 24:23). So here you have it: initially God chooses. Then you are admonished to choose him. This makes sense: the greater chooses the lesser. In any adoption, the parent chooses the child. Then, hopefully, the child reciprocates by choosing to love and obey the parent.

Record what you have learned from reading these passages.

How can you justify your position with Scripture? Give examples.

You can choose to cooperate with God's choice, or not. A rebellious Christian is a miserable person: pathetic, disobedient, and distant from a loving heavenly Father. Why would anyone want to be disobedient? I can answer only for myself. I chose to disobey God by marrying an unbeliever. The cause of that sin was the same as an earlier sin: not trusting God. Rather than choosing confession and repentance, I turned not trusting him into an act of greater disobedience by trying to redeem myself through marriage.

God's grace and love are so magnificent and so available that you do not need to try to redeem yourself, an act that you cannot accomplish in any case. May I encourage all who read this to run to him, not away from him. God has chosen you. You may run to him and ask for forgiveness any time. He will give his children whatever they need and often will give things they want. Take every possible opportunity to talk to him about anything and everything. Ask him for anything you want. He may or may not give it to you, but the asking will always be better than not asking, and you stay closer to him.

Do you think God wants you to know him intimately?

Do you want to know him intimately? Does that question make you uncomfortable? If so, do you know why? What do you have to confess?

The Goal

The goal of this chapter has been to help you develop a desire for intimacy with God and to have a better understanding of who he is. In today's world of evil, noise, and clutter, God offers you the choice of intimacy with him. It requires some effort on your part: praying about everything, studying his Word, and internalizing parts of the Bible that are personally meaningful to you. You can both be and feel safe and loved with him. Isaiah 41:10 and 13 say that he is holding your right hand with his right hand. *Your right hands are clasped.* Knowing you are loved and forgiven is the most restorative power on earth. That will be covered further in chapter 12. Christianity is not always easy, but it is always simple. He will never leave you or forsake you. Living a life of intimacy with God is very rewarding because

It Really Is All About Him.

2

CREATED BY HIM

Why Was I Born?
I Wanted To Know.

> Then God said, "Let us [Father, Son and Holy Spirit] make mankind in our image, after our likeness ... So God created man in his own image, in the image and likeness of God He created him; male and female He created them."
> —Genesis 1:26a, 27 (AB)

What Is an Image?

An *image* is defined as "a reproduction ... of a person; exact likeness; a tangible or visible representation; a person strikingly like another person."[5] *Vine's Concise Dictionary of the Bible* says in 1 Corinthians 11:7 that you are to be "a visible representation of God."[6] O'Collins and Farrugia state, "Human beings, male and female, were created in the divine image and likeness" of God.[7]

These definitions say I am to be strikingly like Jesus, a visible representation. That is quite a challenge. Also, since Christ was a physical

---

[5]   *Merriam-Webster's Collegiate Dictionary*, 11th ed., s.v. "image."
[6]   W. E. Vine, *Vine's Concise Dictionary of the Bible*, s.v. "image."
[7]   G. S. O'Collins and E. G. Farrugia, *Concise Dictionary of Theology*, s.v. "image."

man, you might wonder how this applies to women. Galatians 3:28 says that in Christ there is no difference between male and female: we are all one in Christ. Our likeness to Christ is not gender specific. Men and women are both to be strikingly like Jesus. I will be using *man* generically, including both men and women.

Why Was I Born?

I was created *to be an exact likeness or visible representation of Jesus*. Wow. That is why I was born!

What happened?

It seems Satan could not stand all the beauty and perfection in the Garden of Eden since it was not centered on him. (This is my assumption, not stated in Scripture.) After a brief conversation with Eve (the woman God had created to be a helper to Adam), during which Satan questioned and lied about God's instruction, Eve fell for his deception. (See *It's All about Him* for the significance of being a helper [Brittell 2014, 13–14]). This changed the course of human history. Adam and Eve engaged in the first act of disobedience. Their disobedience resulted in the ultimate death of all life on this earth. The whole story is recorded in Genesis 3. Take time to read it. It reflects the beginning of all life on this earth.

Before their act of disobedience, they could have lived forever. There was no prohibition against eating from the Tree of Life in the center of the garden. Think about that for a moment: living in a perfect environment forever. In reality, you cannot even imagine what that might have been like. The rest of the Bible is an account of how God made it possible for people to live forever again in a perfect environment. Only this time, the consequence of disobedience means that while all people will live forever, only some will live in a perfect environment.

As part of their punishment, Adam and Eve were sent out of the garden. Satan and the ground were cursed; Adam and Eve were each assigned specific punishments. Death entered the world for the first time. The consequences, including death, continue to this day. After the fall, everything eventually dies: people, plants, and animals. In addition, Satan has now become the god of this world. What disastrous results occurred from a brief conversation with the Devil! In any conversation between a person and Satan, the human always loses something of value, often a thing of eternal value.

What were the punishments for each of them (Genesis 3:14–19)?

How do they relate to your life?

Does this mean that all was lost in creation? No, God had declared that everything he had made was good. How then to rescue the whole planet from the grip of Satan? God designed a plan of redemption that was activated after Adam and Eve ate the fruit. The plan included eternal punishment for Satan and the opportunity for salvation for the people of the earth. The plan is referred to in Genesis 3:15. Although it would take thousands of years to be fulfilled with the life, death, resurrection, and ascension of Jesus Christ, it is still in force. You are still living according to the rules initiated by God at that time. Most of us will die, except those who are alive and remain at his second coming (1 Corinthians 5:22). However, death is not the final word.

How do you feel at this point?

After Adam and Eve's disobedience, a whole new plan called redemption was put in place. Even though most people will eventually die a natural death, we will all be raised to eternal life. God designed a plan through which all people can live forever, as he had originally intended. The great difference is that just as Adam and Eve were cast out of the garden, those who choose not to believe God will forever be denied the opportunity to live with him in a perfect environment called heaven. They will be consigned to a place of eternal torture apart from God, called hell.

One of the early consequences of the fall was that real, physical death occurred. Animals were killed to provide clothing for Adam and Eve. Before their disobedience, they were naked but felt no shame. After disobeying, they felt shame. There is no record that their shame led them to repent or feel sorrow. Currently, God grants us the opportunity to feel shame or sorrow for our disobedience through the convicting work of his Holy Spirit. The Spirit's presence within us came much later in the course of history.

What feelings do you have about Adam and Eve?

What do you feel about Satan? Does the entire account make you want to avoid Satan and his influence?

Image Bearer: Man Made in the Image of Adam

After the fall, man was now made in the image and likeness of Adam, the first man (1 Corinthians 15). The fragility of his condition, being made of dust, became evident early in history. Interestingly, God talked to Adam, but the serpent spoke to Eve. In 1 Timothy 2:14, Paul points out that the woman was deceived, not the man. However, the man also ate the fruit. In fact, Adam was the first to use the defense mechanism called *projection,* in which one blames others for their weaknesses, misdeeds, or sins (Genesis 3:12). Here was the first opportunity for the husband to protect his wife (Ephesians 5). The image of God in Adam was now marred.

In spite of Satan's best efforts to ruin the whole earth, man was still a beautiful creation. David provides a wonderful description in Psalm 139:13–16. Despite Adam and Eve's disobedience, God continued to make his creation, including people, a thing of beauty.

What are your reactions to those verses?

(In my ponderings, I wonder what would have happened if Adam had refused to eat the fruit offered by Eve. I know it was all part of God's design, so I don't spend a lot of time on it.)

God continued to give gifts to people. Adam and Eve were given children. Noah was given instructions to build the ark. Abraham was given wealth and a beautiful wife (Genesis 12–17). Bezalel and Oholiab were given gifts of creativity in several mediums, including metals and fabrics (Exodus 31). Samson was given hair and strength (Judges 13–16). David was described as being handsome and having beautiful eyes (1 Samuel 16:12). Solomon was given wisdom and wealth (1 Kings 3). Vashti, a queen, was very beautiful. She was described as "lovely to look at" (Esther 1:11). Daniel and his friends were given intellectual gifts of wisdom and learning. Daniel was also given the gift of interpreting dreams (Daniel 1:17). The creation itself was still beautiful in many respects, even though the reflection of God was marred.

Take some time to think about your gifts. What are the gifts God has given you?

Have you thanked him for your body parts: hair, eyes, nose, mouth, voice, form, and height? He chose the genes that resulted in how you look (Psalm 139:13–16). Write some praises for various aspects of your body that you enjoy. They are gifts from God.

He gave me large blue eyes and a short stature, for which I am grateful. In a retreat at which I was the keynote speaker, I asked the women to publicly thank God for his gifts. One woman thanked God for her form, which was obviously a great gift from God. It took courage to speak of it publicly, but isn't that what praise is about?

Praise him.

Are you artistically, athletically, intellectually, mechanically, or musically gifted? Do you celebrate the gifts, abilities, and talents God has given you? Recognizing these gifts from God and praising him for them will draw you closer to him in intimacy. Remember neither you nor your parents picked these gifts for you. God did!

Write some praises for abilities or talents you have: gifts from God, the Creator of the universe. You may have studied or practiced to fine-tune them, but the inherent abilities are God given.

What are some of your talents?

What does all this mean to you?

Who influences you the most? Whose voice do you recognize most readily, God's or Satan's?

How is Satan causing you to be tempted into disobedience? What similarities do you find between how Satan tempted Adam and Eve and how he tempts you?

If you aren't sure about your temptations, look up the passages in Romans 13:13; 1 Corinthians 6:6, 9–10; Galatians 5:16–24; Ephesians 4:25–5:5; 1 Timothy 1:10–11; and Revelation 21:8 and 22:15 for help identifying some of the ways Satan tries to get you to sin.

What is your greatest vulnerability? Make a list of your greatest temptations.

A Path to Restoration

Look in the dictionary to see what some of those words actually mean. In your concordance, find Scriptures associated with those temptations. You will likely find someone else who was tempted in the same way and what it led to. Remember that Jesus was tempted in every way that you have been tempted (Hebrews 4:15). But he never sinned.

Can you fathom that?

What kept Jesus from sinning? Do you remember the Holy Spirit came down in the form of a dove and rested on him after he was baptized (Luke 3)?

Jesus was empowered by the Holy Spirit. And he knew Scripture. The record of his temptation is in Luke 4. Every time Satan tried to get Jesus to sin, Jesus quoted Scripture. Psalm 119:11 says, "I have stored up your word in my heart, that I might not sin against you." The same things that kept Jesus from sinning are available to you: the power of the Holy Spirit and the Scripture embedded in your heart.

How does it feel to know that the same power that protected Jesus from sinning is available to keep you from sinning? That is pretty awesome when you stop and think about it!

Image Bearer: The Spiritual Man

In the previous section, we looked at some characteristics of a natural man or woman. Adam was the model for the natural man. Examining yourself and people in the Bible gives some idea of what a natural person is. Since you are both body (natural) and spirit (spiritual), let's look at being made in the image of God from a spiritual perspective.

27

Jesus, the Christ, is the model for the spiritual man. He was both fully man and fully God. Take some time to reflect on that in terms of his birth and how you celebrate Christmas.

Jesus became a human person, a physically natural man, born via the natural birth process through Mary. He had always been a spiritual being in heaven before he came down to earth. Philippians 2:6–11 tells how he left his home in heaven to put on a human form. This passage gives us the whole plan of salvation in abbreviated form: the holy Son of God left his celestial home to live in Bethlehem, Egypt, and Nazareth as the son of a carpenter. He lived, died, rose again, and ascended to heaven, where he invites his children to join him. His humility will be addressed again in a later chapter.

Record your thoughts.

How do we move from being natural people, male and female, to being spiritual people? We do the opposite of what Jesus did: Jesus was a spiritual person who became a human; we are human people who become spiritual people when we are born again. The term *born again* makes sense. You become a natural person through your first birth, a spiritual person through your second birth.

> The first man Adam became a living being; the last Adam became a life-giving spirit. But it is not the spiritual that is first but the natural, and then the spiritual. The first man was from the earth, a man of dust, so also are those who are of the dust, and as the man of heaven, so also are those who are of heaven. Just as we have borne the image of the man of dust, we shall also bear the image of the man of heaven.
>
> —1 Corinthians 15:45–49

How Does This Happen?

You have been redeemed. Jesus has redeemed you. To *redeem* means to buy back or to be freed from captivity.[8] Vine says "to redeem … indicates some intervening or substitutionary action effects a release from an undesirable condition; save from death."[9] O'Collins and Farrugia say that a *redeemer* is "one who pays to liberate somebody."[10]

Christ came to earth and became a human in order to redeem you: to buy you back from being controlled by Satan. God made all this possible to reverse the effect of what Satan had done in the garden. With a question and a beautiful tree, Satan tried to undo all that God had done: small temptations bore huge consequences. Once Adam and Eve had been disobedient and eaten the fruit, they could no longer represent the glory of God. Satan had now become the god of this world. They had given their dominion over the earth to Satan.

God, the Father, asked Jesus, the Son, to come to earth as a human being to die on the cross to redeem you: to buy you back from Satan's control. What an enormous eternal event: Christ gave his life for you so that you would not have to be bound by Satan! With a simple piece of fruit, the Devil tried to undo all that God had created. Undoing what Satan had done required the death and resurrection of Christ. Satan dealt with just two people. Christ's death and resurrection redeemed multitudes of people.

What are you feeling and thinking as you absorb all this?

Have you accepted what Jesus has done for you? Writing your response will help solidify your thoughts.

Paul, in 1 Corinthians 6:11, describes the process of redemption as having been washed, sanctified, and justified "in the name of the Lord

---

[8]   *Merriam-Webster's Collegiate Dictionary*, 11th ed., s.v. "redeem."
[9]   *Vine's Concise Dictionary*, s.v. "redeem."
[10] O'Collins and Farrugia, *Concise Dictionary of Theology*, s.v. "redeemer."

Jesus Christ and by the Spirit of our God." *Sanctification* means to be set apart for holiness. To be *justified* is to be made righteous before God. Both of these huge gifts take place as a result of Christ's death and resurrection. If you are unclear as to the meanings of these two words, look them up in the dictionary and your concordance.

Whoever has accepted what Christ has done for them in his death and resurrection is now a spiritual person. You have had a second birth; you have now become a Christian. You now have eternal life with God and a new nature. God no longer keeps a record of your sin. How good is that? The image of God that was to have been reflected by Adam, but was marred, can now reflect his glory through you.

What is the glory of God? In a church I once attended, I was taught that *glory* meant light; that is, to shine a light on God. The dictionary broadens that meaning and my understanding of the glory of God. Some of the words used *by Merriam-Webster's* include *great beauty and splendor, renown, magnificence, something marked by beauty or resplendence, light.*[11] This results in much more praise.

Vine says glory is used in the self-manifestation of God, "particularly in the person of Christ."[12] His glory is evident in the "character and acts" of Christ, in his power and grace. Some of the acts of his glory include raising Lazarus from the dead, being raised from the dead himself, being transfigured, and creating everything. His glory is especially evident in his character of righteousness and perfection. In Ephesians 1:17–19, Paul prays that the Father of glory will give us a spirit of wisdom … and hope … and enlightenment of the glorious inheritance that is ours in Christ and awareness of the "greatness of his power toward us who believe." O'Collins and Farrugia state that in the Old Testament, the glory of God was "the majestic radiance manifesting God's presence."[13]

Is this what you thought the glory of God meant? How does this meaning change your understanding of the glory of God? Record your reactions so you can go back to them as often as you need to.

---

[11] *Merriam-Webster's Collegiate Dictionary*, 11th ed., s.v. "glory."

[12] *Vine's Concise Dictionary*, s.v. "glory."

[13] O'Collins and Farrugia, *Concise Dictionary of Theology*, s.v. "glory."

All of this is an act of *grace*, which means undeserved favor. You don't deserve any of these good things because we all have the desire and tendency to be disobedient, just like Adam and Eve. Before we become spiritual people, before we are born again, we want to be just as disobedient as Adam and Eve. Sometimes our upbringing or a threat of punishment keeps us from acting out, but the desire is always present in the old nature.

After all, how big a deal is it to eat one piece of forbidden fruit?

In 1 Corinthians 15:49, Paul says that just as we looked like "the man of dust," Adam, we shall look like the "man of heaven," Jesus. Your ability to be transformed into the image of Christ "from one degree of glory to another" comes from the Holy Spirit (2 Corinthians 3:18).

Paul, in Romans 7 and Galatians 5:16–25, writes eloquently about the ongoing war between the old nature and the new nature, between the natural man (the flesh) and the spiritual man.

> For the desires of the flesh are against the desires of the Spirit, and the desires of the Spirit are against the flesh, for they are opposed to each other, to keep you from doing the things you want to do.
>
> —Galatians 5:17

What are some of the ways in which Satan tempts you symbolically to eat just one piece of forbidden fruit? Write a paragraph, just for your own learning experience, about a time when you yielded to temptation.

Then write about the impact of the consequences.

What did you learn from the experience?

You can go back to the passages suggested in an earlier paragraph to help you identify your areas of vulnerability. My areas of vulnerability have been anxiety and detachment; both are manifestations of anxiety. God says to not be anxious. Therefore, anxiety is sin. I write more about this in chapter 7. Once you have been born again of the Spirit, find a Bible-believing church. Pray to find good Christian friends. I was blessed: I was raised in a strong Christian family, church, and high school where I developed strong Christian friendships.

Who are your Christian supports? Your peers can be very important to growing in Christ.

God was so good. He gave me a group of strong Christian girlfriends who became strong Christian women friends. Our group reflects the image of Christ in amazingly different ways. One was a missionary, one a hospital chaplain, two were teachers, one a teacher's aide, one was the head of the neonatal department in a large hospital, and I became a licensed psychologist. Each of us reflects the image of God differently.

Look at your group of close friends. How does each one reflect Christ?

How do they help you grow in your faith in Christ? If they do not, pray for guidance in finding new friends.

You Have Been Adopted

Once redeemed, you are adopted into the family of God. Paul says in Ephesians 1:5, "In love he predestined us for adoption as sons through Jesus Christ, according to the purpose of his will." Think about that for a few minutes. When you are born, you don't even know about God. When you are born again, he adopts you as his child. Pretty awesome, isn't it?

What does adoption mean?

It means that your spiritual birth certificate shows God's name. God is your Father. You belong to God's family spiritually, psychologically, and physically. Your name is written in his book of life.

You are now called a *temple* of the Holy Spirit. There are five references that speak to the fact that you have been *bought* by Jesus and are now *owned* by God. Look them up and study them.

- You are a temple: 1 Corinthians 3:16.
- You have been bought by God: 1 Corinthians 6:19–20.
- You have been bought with a price: 1 Corinthians 7:23.
- You are sealed with the promised Holy Spirit: Ephesians 1:13–14.
- You have been redeemed to be a possession for God: Titus 2:14 and Revelation 5:9.

Jesus bought you with his blood. Sin no longer has control over you; you are in God's family. He has adopted you. The Holy Spirit lives in your body; he has been given to you as a seal of belonging to God's family (Ephesians 1:13). Understanding this may require some time and effort. Take time to internalize it. Then write your reactions.

The Holy Spirit now lives inside each born-again person. Some of his functions include teaching you, helping you, comforting you, convicting you of sin, and reminding you of what Jesus taught. As you let the Holy Spirit guide you into truth, your behavior will likely change. This new behavior is called the *fruit of the Spirit* (Galatians 5:22–23).

Following is a list of the fruit and its meaning. Look them up in your concordance, write down some of the verses that apply to each of them, and see how they were used in the New Testament.

- *love*: a deep, tender feeling of affection, a commitment, godly action
- *joy*: rejoicing, happiness, great pleasure, delight, contentment, gladness
- *peace*: absence of mental conflict, freedom from quarrels, harmony, a state of tranquility
- *patience*: refusing to be angered, able to wait calmly, enduring without complaint
- *kindness*: sympathy, friendliness, generosity, tenderheartedness, being considerate
- *goodness*: respectability, moral excellence, devotion, honesty, virtuousness, generosity
- *faithfulness*: steadfast, loyalty, reliability, trustworthiness
- *gentleness*: courteousness, serenity, having an amiable nature, without harshness or loudness
- *self-control*: control of oneself, including one's emotions, thoughts, and actions; ability to regulate, restrain, and govern oneself

Jesus lived the fruit of the Spirit. Look up and record at least one example of Jesus manifesting each fruit of the Spirit in his interactions with people.

Remember the Holy Spirit had come down on him in the shape of a dove following his baptism. Most of us won't have doves confirming our filling with the Spirit, but you will begin to realize you are making Christian choices in your lifestyles.

Write down some of the changes you see occurring in your own life.

How do you feel about those changes?

Because you now have a new nature, a spiritual one, it often feels as though there is a battle going on inside you between the new spiritual nature and the old natural nature. Sometimes it feels very much like a war. Paul, in Romans 6–8, talks at some length about the war between your two natures. He uses the example of slavery as a model. When you were under the control of Satan, you were his slave and lived in sin. Now you have become a slave of righteousness. Paul also asks what benefit you received from the old behavior.

Write down some of the old behavior in which you used to engage.

What, if any, benefit did you get from these activities?

What regrets do you have regarding any of them?

What consequences, either positive or negative, have followed these behaviors?

Have you asked for forgiveness for having caused God or others pain with these behaviors? If so, God has forgiven you. Do you need to ask for forgiveness from someone else? Psalm 51 is a great example of David asking for forgiveness.

Transforming Your Mind

While the above characteristics are the result of the Holy Spirit living within you, you can also cooperate with him in developing these traits in yourself. You can always cooperate with God to become the person he wants you to be. Learning to take control of your thoughts can be most helpful in letting the Holy Spirit guide you. In Romans 12:2, the Lord commands us to "be transformed by the renewing of our mind." In 2 Corinthians 10:5, Paul says you are to take your thoughts captive to Christ. Isaiah 26:3–4 says that keeping your mind on him will bring you peace. The Lord wants it to be obvious that you have been transformed from being controlled by Satan to being controlled by the Holy Spirit.

Following are a number of questions designed to help you learn to think about God first in everyday experiences. Read the questions carefully and meditate on those that apply to you. This section is taken largely from the original book, *It's All about Him* (Brittell 2014, 9–11).

How tall are you? He picked your genetic code. "You knitted me together in my mother's womb. I praise you, for I am fearfully and wonderfully made" (Psalm 139:13–14). Do you praise him for your height?

Do you have talents? He gave you those talents. They are part of his forming you in the womb (Psalm 139:15). Do you praise him for the talents?

Do you like jewelry? When you wear your jewelry, do you think of God? He created the original stones and the gold, silver, platinum, or brass (Genesis 2:12).

Has someone you loved died? That is about Him. "Precious in the sight of the Lord is the death of his saints" (Psalm 116:15).

A Path to Restoration

Each one of us has a certain number of days to live, allotted by God before our birth. "In your book were written, every one of them, the days that were formed for me, when as yet there was none of them" (Psalm 139:16). What are your thoughts?

Have you been disobedient? You were disobeying the Lord. "I have sinned against the Lord" (2 Samuel 12:13). "Against you, you only, have I sinned and done what is evil in your sight" (Psalm 51:4). Have you asked God's forgiveness?

Have you been obedient? Again, you were obeying the Lord. He made all the original rules. "We destroy arguments and every lofty opinion raised against the knowledge of God, and take every thought captive to obey Christ" (2 Corinthians 10:5). Have you praised him for the grace to resist temptation?

Do you have disabilities or chronic illness sometimes called a "thorn in the flesh" (2 Corinthians 12:7)? They are about God, even though they may have come through birth, illness, or accident. However, he causes all things to work together for good to those who love him and are called according to his purpose (Romans 8:28).

Have you tried to stop breathing? God picked the day of your death before you were born (Psalm 139:16). Have you ever thought of suicide as a solution? He has grace enough to help you overcome whatever you are struggling with. Don't try to override his choice.

Are you artistic (Exodus 31:1–6)? Do you love color? He has set the color spectrum at creation as part of creating light. You can rearrange amounts of color to make new combinations, but you cannot create new color out of nothing. Do you enjoy creating things?

Are you inclined toward engineering? At creation God created sound and electromagnetic waves, such as TV, microwaves, and X-rays. Do you work with any of these?

Are you mechanically inclined? Did you change a tire or the oil in your car recently? Humans invented these things, but God created all the raw materials and gave people the wisdom to put it all together (Job 38:36)

What do you eat? He created all the original food (Genesis 1:13, 24). Do you regard your food as a gift from God?

What do you drink? He created water (Genesis 1:2, 6, 9). We have polluted it. However, he made pure water, sometimes miraculously (Exodus 17:6).

Are you redeemed? Christ died for your salvation (John 3:16). To redeem means to buy back. Have you been bought back from the control of Satan?

Are you resisting salvation? If you are resisting salvation, you are resisting God. "Who are you, O man, to answer back to God?" (Romans 9:20)

Do you like the seasons? He made them.

> And God said, "Let there be lights in the expanse of the heavens to separate the day from the night, and let them be for signs and for seasons, and for days and years, and let them be lights in the expanse of the heavens to give light upon the earth." And it was so.
>
> —Genesis 1:14–15

What is your favorite season? What do you enjoy most about it?

Do you think you know another's motives? You don't. God does. "For the Lord searches all hearts and understands every plan and thought" (1 Chronicles 28:9).

How do you know the difference between right and wrong? He gave both the Ten Commandments (Exodus 20) and the Holy Spirit to convict people of sin. "He will convict the world concerning sin" (John 16:8). Do you recognize the voice of the Holy Spirit?

Are you born again? If so, the Holy Spirit has been given you as a seal (2 Corinthians 1:22; Ephesians 1:13). He lives in you. Your body is his temple (1 Corinthians 3:16; 6:19). Wherever you go, the Holy Spirit inside you, goes too.

Have you given birth? Did you have labor pains? They came from God via Eve (Genesis 3).

If you are a man, have you had to work by the sweat of your brow or under stress? That came from God via Adam (Genesis 3).

Are your relationships about him? Do they bring him glory? "Do not be unequally yoked" (2 Corinthians 6:14).

How many kinds of pens do you have on your desk or dishes in your cupboards? How many kinds of wood or fabric do you have in your home? How many electronic gadgets or tools? Do you stop to think that he created the materials and formulas for making everything in the universe?

Did you measure something to cook, bake, build, or plant recently? "A just balance and scales are the Lords; all the weights in the bag are his work" (Proverbs 16:11).

Did you wash dishes or windows recently? He made all the sand out of which the glass is made.

I recently reflected on some silk lampshades in my home. I know silk comes from silkworms. I am not usually fond of worms of any kind. Then I began to think about God's gift of silk. I had to change my thought pattern. I had to take my thoughts captive and let them be renewed by

God to be grateful for worms. You need to do this with any thoughts that do not honor him.

What things do you like? Some of my favorite things are shoes, food, jewel tones, cool or cold weather, books, heaven, forgiveness, and the coast. These are all bases for generating praise to God. They will all help me stay at peace when I relate each of them to God.

These ideas can help you learn to take your thoughts captive in order to be transformed by the renewing of your mind. The more you are thinking about God and what would please Him, the more you will be at peace. Start looking around your life for ways to transform your thoughts so you are always thinking about him first, praising him, and reflecting him. Learn to enjoy the peace that will come into your mind. As you become more sensitive to his love and presence, your brain chemistry may begin to change. It is actually possible in today's technological world to see a brain scan that shows the changes in your brain as your processes change. God said to be transformed by the renewing of our minds. Now you can see it happen on a scan.

God says to pray without ceasing (1 Thessalonians 5:17). You could do that just by praising him for all he has done for you and has created for your enjoyment. Start making your own list. Update it often. Develop the habit of thinking about him as your mind takes in any new thought.

The Goal

The goal of this chapter has been to help you see what it means to be made in the image of God. Although the image was marred by Adam and Eve's sin, you have been granted the gift of redemption (deliverance). As a result, you have the privilege of being born again, being adopted into God's family.

This chapter also explains that you have two natures: the old one that sin controls and the new one that the Holy Spirit controls, if you have been born again. It describes the behavior that reflects the new nature: love, joy, peace, patience, kindness, goodness, faithfulness, gentleness, and self-control. God knew before the foundation of the world that he wanted to adopt you. You are now his child. There is no more secure position in the whole universe than to be purchased by God. Can he return, send, or give you back? He says no. "I give them eternal life, and they will never perish, and no one will *snatch* them out of my hand" (John 10:28, emphasis added). When you are born again, no thing can separate you from the love of God in Christ Jesus:

> Who shall separate us from the love of Christ? Shall tribulation, or distress, or persecution, or famine, or nakedness, or danger, or sword? … For I am sure that neither death nor life, nor angels nor rulers, nor things present nor things to come, nor powers, nor height nor depth, nor anything else in all creation, will be able to separate us from the love of God in Christ Jesus, our Lord.
>
> —Romans 8:35, 38–39

You Have Been Created In His Image

You Have Been Redeemed

3

IDENTITY IN HIM

Who am I?
I wanted to know.

For you formed my inward parts; you knitted me together in my mother's womb. I praise you, for I am fearfully and wonderfully made.

—Psalm 139:13

I am someone whom God made. He chose my varied parts.

All seven billion of us are fearfully and wonderfully made. You often say, "Oh, that person looks so much like whomever you think they resemble." Physical traits are passed down through our genes.

How do our spiritual traits become identifiable? How do you develop an identity in Christ? How do you develop a spiritual identity?

What Is an Identity?

Identity means oneness or sameness with an objective reality of a thing.[14] It means there are characteristics that are identifiable as belonging to a certain thing—in this case, a person.

In his human nature, Jesus was of Jewish descent. Mary, his mother, was a Jewess. In his divine nature, he was like his Father, Jehovah. John 17 often mentions the oneness between Jesus and his Father. Jesus prays that you, God's child, will become part of that oneness. You are to be similar to Jesus once you have been born again. He has redeemed you: bought you back from slavery to sin. You can now identify with Jesus in your body. He had the same kind of body as other men.

How You Look Is Part of Your Identity

How do you look? Are you short or tall, round or slim? Are you blonde, brunet, red, or white haired? What physical characteristics are prominent in your body? What features do people see and say, "Oh, you look just like whomever"?

Write about your physical characteristics.

Jesus was descended from his Father. You, too, are descended from your father. Your father carried your life seed in his body. When your life began in your mother's womb, God took genes from each of your parents to create you. Psalm 139 speaks beautifully of the process that led to your design. It is part of your identity. Whether you are tall or short, round or slim, blonde, brunet, red, or white haired makes a difference in how you see and interact with the world. Your design is unique to you. In midlife, I changed my hair color from brunette to blonde. My identity changed. The description on my driver's license changed. People interacted with me differently. One of my friends identified me on one occasion as the blonde in the balcony.

Make some notes about how your body looks that sets you apart from your siblings and other members of your family. List two or three

---

14   *Merriam-Webster's Collegiate Dictionary*, 11th ed., s.v. "identity."

God-given, genetic characteristics that make you unique. Remember they are God given. He wanted you to have them. Neither you nor your parents chose them: God did.

As you read in the last chapter, God has used physical beauty to bring glory to himself. List some people whose beauty he used to influence the world.

Your Gifts Are Part of Your Identity

The natural gifts God gave you are also part of your identity. Whether you are gifted in artistic, athletic, creative, intellectual, mechanical, musical, or other ways makes a difference in how you interact with the world. Your talents are part of your identity. If you deny that you have talents, you are denying that God has given you abilities. You are denying a part of his goodness.

List some of the natural abilities and talents God has given you. Do you recognize they are gifts? You did absolutely nothing to get them. Once you realized you were gifted, you may have worked to develop them, but initially they were gifts from God. Isn't it amazing that he would give us gifts, just for his, our, and others' enjoyment?

How are you using your gifts to glorify either God or yourself?

Whether you have sufficient financial resources can make a difference in how you see your identity. Great poverty or great wealth can have an impact on how you perceive your sense of yourself. Both can be burdensome. With great wealth often comes a sense of arrogance, pride, or entitlement. With great poverty often comes a sense of hopelessness and despair. How you choose to use either your wealth or your poverty or to rise above it and use your God-given gifts and talents can make a difference in your identity. A wonderful passage in Proverbs addresses these conditions. "Give me neither poverty nor riches … lest I be full and deny you … or lest I be poor and steal and profane the name of my God" (Proverbs 30:8–9). Knowing that your Father in heaven has all the wealth in the world can help you maintain equilibrium whatever your circumstance (Psalm 50:10–12).

Whether or not you are in an environment that supports and encourages you and helps you develop your abilities can make a great difference to your identity. Christ's family wanted to take charge of him because they thought he had lost his mind (Mark 3:21). Christ knew who he was, so what his family thought of him didn't really matter. He did not have a bed to sleep in. Yet all the wealth in the world is his.

Think of and write down some of the people in the culture who have risen to great fame from great poverty. Let this list encourage you if you come from meager means.

Take some time to think about how you see yourself. Do you know who you are? Make notes to help you cement these concepts in your mind.

What Is Your Identity?

The preceding can be seen as identity issues. However, the most important identity issue is whether or not you belong to God. If you have been born again, you are a child of God, a son or daughter of the King of Kings, a prince or princess in God's kingdom. You have been purchased by the death and resurrection of the Lord, Jesus Christ. You are a prized person, a purchased one. You have been adopted into the family of God (Ephesians 1:5).

Chapter 2 speaks of your having been purchased by Jesus's blood. There is no greater method of exchange than Jesus's blood: His righteousness in exchange for your sin and His death in exchange for your life. God loved you so much that he has done the following:

- He gave his only begotten Son to save you so you can have everlasting life (John 3:16).
- He forgave your sins (Ephesians 1:7). He redeemed you: he bought you back from Satan's control (Ephesians 2:2–9).
- He predestined you for adoption to ensure that you would be part of his family forever (Ephesians 1:5, 11).
- He is building you into a "dwelling place" for the Holy Spirit to live in (Ephesians 2:22).
- He has given his Spirit to live in you. "Do you not know that you are God's *temple*, and that God's Spirit dwells in you?" (1 Corinthians 3:16, emphasis added).
- He loves your body. "Or do you not know that your body is a *temple* of the Holy Spirit within you, whom you have from God? You are not your own, for you were *bought* with a price. So glorify God in your *body*" (1 Corinthians 6:19–20, emphasis added).
- "You were *bought* with a price; do not become slaves of men" (1 Corinthians 7:23, emphasis added). Remember whose you are.
- "Who gave himself for us to *redeem* us from all lawlessness and to purify for himself a people for his own possession *who are zealous for good works*" (Titus 2:14, emphasis added). He planned things for you to do.
- "By your blood you *ransomed* [redeemed] people for God from every tribe and language and people and nation" (Revelation 5:9, emphasis added). He bought you with his own blood.

The preceding gives you some idea of how much he loves you.

Let yourself meditate on this for a while. Go to a quiet place to focus on these facts. The idea of an exchange of this magnitude—his life for all our sin, the penalty for all our sin for his righteousness—is just short of overwhelming. If it is overwhelming, let yourself get lost in the wonder of it all. Record your thoughts.

How Can I Live out My New Identity?

Once you have been born again, you have become a temple in which the Holy Spirit lives. God now owns your heart, mind, soul, and body. All of you! There is no part of you that God does not own.

Does that seem scary? Reflect on your feelings and make notes of them. It will be interesting for you to reread the notes as you grow in intimacy with God. What may seem scary now may, in time, become the very awareness that gives you a sense of security at some later point.

When you were born, you were ruled by sin because you were born spiritually dead "in trespasses and sin" (Ephesians 2:1–5). That seems hard to believe when you look at a newborn infant. But this happened to all of us who were born after Adam and Eve ate the fruit in Eden. You were born with a sin nature. You were condemned to die in your sin. Until … Jesus. He provided the intervention that keeps you from being condemned to death. That is what he did when he died on the cross. He took the penalty for yours and everyone's sin.

Taking the penalty for your sin is called atonement. *Atonement* means "to cover over, atone, propitiate, pacify," to be forgiven or wiped away.[15] He paid the price for your sin. Three days after his death, he rose from the dead. Before he ascended back to heaven where he had come from, he told his disciples he would not leave them as orphans but would come to them (John 14:18). When Jesus went to heaven after his resurrection, the Holy Spirit came down from God to live in all who are his children (Acts 2).

---

[15] *Vine's Concise Dictionary*, s.v. "atonement."

The Holy Spirit has been called the Helper (John 14:16). He has been given to you to help you come into the fullness of your identity. John 14–16 lists the following ways in which he helps you:

- comforting you
- teaching you
- reminding you of what Jesus said
- convicting you of sin
- empowering you to live abundantly
- guiding you
- glorifying Jesus

That is a lot of provision. Not many, if any, of your needs fall outside these categories. I have needed all of them at some time in my life. The Holy Spirit ministers to you in many ways according to your needs. God will supply all your needs according to Philippians 4:19. Take some time to look at your own needs. You will need a lot of help to live out your new identity abundantly.

How many ways can you recall in which the Holy Spirit has helped you?

The Holy Spirit uses many means to help you. The Bible is the best and most effective way of providing you with guidance. It is God's Word. This guidance can come through your own study, which I highly recommend. If you have limited time to read and study, focus on the Bible. The Lord tells us to study to show ourselves approved in handling the scripture (2 Timothy 2:15). Pastors, teachers, or counselors can help. Sometimes God will minister to you through nature and through meditating on him and his words. He may give you visions and dreams. This happened several times in the Old Testament when the Holy Spirit had not yet been given to all the Israelites. Sometimes the Holy Spirit will speak to you directly.

Make notes of times and circumstances in which the Holy Spirit helped you by using any of these methods.

I came to the point of wanting to learn to hear and recognize the voice of the Holy Spirit more clearly than anyone else's. For a year, I spent one day a week sitting in the same chair with the intended goal of learning to recognize his voice. I had my Bible open and would turn to passages I felt he was directing me to read. I asked him to speak to me. *He did.* At the end of that year, I could recognize his voice for eight hours at a time. He says his sheep hear his voice (John 10:27). There is more on that year in chapter 12 where it speaks of my restoration. "If you seek him, he will be found by you" (1 Chronicles 28:9).

Have you learned to recognize his voice? Take some time to meditate on where you are in your ability to hear and learn from the Holy Spirit. *This is a crucial element* in your maturing into your new identity. Note any areas where you feel uncertain of the Holy Spirit's work in your life. If you need help in clarifying some issues, ask for it. The Holy Spirit will guide you to someone who can help you.

Is It Obvious That the Holy Spirit Is Controlling Your Life?

In the last chapter, I introduced you to the fruit of the Holy Spirit as listed in Galatians 5:22. It can be useful and helpful to look at it again. Below is a list of the fruit of the Spirit and some opposites.

Fruit of the Spirit	Opposites
• love	anger, hate, rage, murder
• joy	anger, depression, complaining
• peace	anxiety, agitation, restlessness
• patience	annoyance, irritability
• kindness	meanness, rudeness, viciousness
• goodness	evil in any form
• faithfulness	deceit, betrayal, criticalness
• gentleness	harshness, roughness, criticalness
• self-control	impulsivity, rashness, acting out

The fruit of the Spirit should be a part of every Christian's identity. Do not fear letting the Holy Spirit control your life. He already lives in you. He is given to you as a seal of your salvation when you are born again. All the expressions of the presence of the Spirit are acts of love. Isn't it better to be kind rather than mean and gentle rather than critical? This is to be an automatic part of how you live. Fruit emerges from what is within. It doesn't stress and strain. Trees don't groan and stress to produce fruit. It happens automatically if the tree is cultivated, fed, and watered.

Being filled with the Spirit should result in the simple awareness of letting him guide your life, your existence, constantly. This will result in fruit. You are to be fed through the study of God's Word. Water represents the Holy Spirit. If you are internalizing God's Word and submitting to the Holy Spirit, you will be bearing fruit.

Look in the dictionary to see what these opposite words really mean.

Ask the Spirit to convict you when you have engaged in any of the opposites. Then repent and ask for forgiveness. If you see yourself habitually engaging in any of these opposite attitudes or behaviors, check your commitment to God and to your own well-being. If you cherish any of these, Psalm 66:18 says the Lord will not hear, much less answer, your prayer. He has made it so simple—not necessarily easy, but simple. Ask the Holy Spirit to guide your life daily or hourly and to convict you where necessary. Better to be convicted and repent than to continue in sin and have to live with the consequences.

Do you want to live with the Holy Spirit in control of your life? If not, why not?

The Gifts of the Spirit

Earlier I referred to God's omnipotence: his power. His power is such that he created the universe by the power of his word. Isn't that totally amazing?

He said a word or words and the universe came into being. That is power that you and I have never had. You can only see the results of smashing atoms or the booster rockets that send thousands of pounds of material and people into space. You see the results of powerful events in which God has allowed man to participate. However, you cannot create anything out of nothing.

God, in his grace, created things for you to do, works that he had chosen for you before you were created (Ephesians 2:10). Then he gives you the power of the Holy Spirit, which is his power, to perform them. The most significant reason for these gifts is to give him glory. There are many ways to accomplish this. Worshipping and praising him are two ways that give him glory. When you use any and all the talents he has given you, he will be pleased and glorified.

In addition to natural talents and abilities, God has given each of his children spiritual, supernatural gifts to be used to help all of his children grow in faith and to build each other up. These are referred to as the gifts of the Spirit. They are supernatural. You can use them only through the power of the Holy Spirit.

The gifts (1 Corinthians 12:8–10) are listed along with definitions and examples of the gifts used in biblical circumstances. Take some time to look at these and spend time reflecting on how they were used. All definitions in this section are taken from A. J. VanderGriend, *Discover Your Gifts and Learn How to Use them* (Grand Rapids, MI: CRC Publications, 1996).

The first gift of *wisdom* is defined as "the special Spirit-given ability to see situations and issues from God's perspective and to apply God-given insights to specific areas of need" (p. 141). Here is an example of supernatural wisdom. There was a man named Simeon, "and the Holy Spirit was upon him" (Luke 2:25). The Holy Spirit showed Simeon that he would not die until he had seen "the Lord's Christ" (Luke 2:26). When Jesus's parents brought the Christ child into the temple to do the prescribed purification, Simeon took Jesus in his arms and pronounced a profound blessing on him.

> Lord, now you are letting your servant depart in peace, according to your word; for my eyes have seen your salvation that you have prepared in the presence of all peoples, a light for revelation to the Gentiles, and for glory to your people Israel.
> —Luke 2:29–32

"And his father and mother marveled at what was said about him" (Luke 2:33). The Holy Spirit gave Simeon words of wisdom. What Simeon said to Mary, "A sword will pierce through your own soul also," can be considered words of prophecy as well (Luke 2:34). What a profound impact these words must have had on these parents. It was a once-in-history event. They *marveled* at the words.

What are your thoughts as you meditate on this event? Take some time to record them.

The next gift mentioned is a *word of knowledge*. Word of knowledge is defined as "the supernatural ability to receive from God knowledge that is crucial to ministry and that could not have been obtained in other ways" (p. 111). A story illustrating this is written of Peter with Ananias and Sapphira (Acts 5:1–11). Peter confronted them with their sin. He knew about their sin (lying) because the Holy Spirit had given him knowledge supernaturally. They dropped dead when confronted. It is fascinating as well as a bit terrifying if you have sin in your life that has not been confessed. The principle is very clear. If you lie to God—to the Holy Spirit—you may have severe consequences.

Revelation 21:8 says that all liars will burn with fire and sulfur. This is the second death. Since the Holy Spirit is called the Spirit of truth, lying is a total affront to that person of the Trinity. He is the one who empowers us to speak the truth. As rejecting Christ's way of salvation through the cross leads to everlasting punishment, so everyone who speaks against the Holy Spirit will not be forgiven in this life or the next (Matthew 12:31). God takes his provision very seriously. It is in our best interest to do the same. (I remember as a child being terrified of telling a lie, lest I, too, should drop dead. By his grace, I am still here.)

What are your reactions to this account?

The next gift is the gift of *faith*. Faith is defined as "the special Spirit-given ability to know with certainty that God wills to do something and is certain to do it, in response to prayer, even when there is no concrete evidence" (p. 91). You often think of faith as part of everyday living. Do you believe in Christ and in his work on the cross? If you have been born again, you would say *yes*. That is called faith. However, the supernatural gift of faith is more specific. It is the firm belief that God is going to do something out of the ordinary in a specific situation. The woman in the story told in Mark 5 had faith that if she just touched Jesus's garment she would be healed of a blood flow that had been going on for twelve years. She did it: she touched his garment and immediately felt in her body "that she was healed of her disease" (Mark 5:29). Jesus said, "Daughter, your faith has made you well; go in peace, and be healed of your disease" (Mark 5:34). The faith she had was a supernatural gift of the Holy Spirit for a specific situation, distinct from everyday faith.

Record your reaction.

Is it all right to ask for gifts? Customarily, we do not ask for gifts. If you ask, it is not a gift. It is the response to a request. Gifts are usually given spontaneously. Would you like a gift from the Holy Spirit? Live in such close communion with Him that he *wants* to give you a gift of his power for his glory.

The next gift is *healing*. Healing is defined as "the special Spirit-given ability to serve as an instrument through whom God brings physical, emotional, and spiritual healing in an extraordinary way (p. 99)." In a wonderful account, the "church throughout all Judea and Galilee and Samaria had peace and was being built up. And walking in the fear of the Lord and in the *comfort* of the Holy Spirit it multiplied" (Acts 9:31, emphasis added). What a wonderful atmosphere. Within this context Peter came to the town of Lydda. There he found a man who had been paralyzed for eight years. He said to the man, "Jesus Christ heals you" (Acts 9:34). The man rose and became a living testimony to God's healing power.

There are many other instances of healing. Look up several and make notes to help you confirm them in your mind. Think of the power it takes to heal someone.

The next gift is *miraculous powers*: "the special Spirit-given ability to serve as an instrument through whom God performs extraordinary works as an expression of his presence and power" (p. 121). Within the same previously mentioned biblical context where Peter performed healing, he raised Dorcas from the dead. There had been much weeping because Dorcas had been a true servant of God. When Peter arrived, he put everyone out of the room, "knelt down and prayed," and told her to get up (Acts 9:40). She did! She was a woman much loved in the community for her good works, so her resurrection caused many to believe in the Lord.

Have you ever wanted to raise someone from the dead? Look into your own heart. Live close to Him. Remember these are gifts given freely by the Holy Spirit to accomplish God's purpose in the world. Make notes of your reactions to this account of what Peter did through the power of the Holy Spirit.

The gift of *prophecy* is "the special Spirit-given ability to receive and communicate a message from God so that believers may be edified and encouraged and so that unbelievers may be convicted" (p. 125). The Old Testament prophets were especially gifted in this manner. They received many messages from God and spoke them to the people. The prophecies included words of warning, comfort, admonition, and prediction, among others.

One of the most outstanding examples of this gift in the New Testament is the prophecy given by Zechariah in Luke 1:68–79. He "was filled with the Holy Spirit" (Luke 1:67) and had just regained his ability to speak. Because he had doubted the word of the angel Gabriel, God's messenger, God made him unable to speak for the nine months of his wife's pregnancy.

Read the prophecy. It is well worth your time. It includes words of praise, comfort, and prediction. It is one of the most comforting passages in scripture. In your own words, write what Zechariah's prophecy predicted. Include the impact it had on you when you read it.

Discerning of spirits is "the special Spirit-given ability to know whether a certain word, action or motive has its source in God, sinful flesh, or Satan" (p. 81). This is a crucial gift because it makes clear that you, even after being born again, can be influenced by evil spirits. You are challenged to "have their [your] powers of discernment trained by constant practice to distinguish good from evil" (Hebrews 5:14). In an account of Jesus casting out an evil spirit, the Pharisees accused him of using the power of Satan to accomplish the deliverance. He, of course, was using the power of the Holy Spirit to set the person free. He stated that whoever spoke against the Holy Spirit would never be forgiven in this life or the next (Matthew 12:32). They were giving to Satan glory that belonged to the Holy Spirit. Jesus said that is unforgiveable, sometimes called the unpardonable sin.

In the course of my years of practice in clinical psychology, I had the opportunity to take training through my church to deliver people from the presence of evil spirits. It was very valuable to be able to discern whether the cause of the problem that was troubling my patient was physical, psychological, or spiritual in origin. Eve tried to get the gift of discernment of good and evil by eating from the forbidden tree in Eden. You know how that worked out. At this time, the Holy Spirit has freely given the gift of discernment to born-again people to bring glory to God and deliverance to his children.

Discernment is a very significant principle in God's kingdom in that giving God the glory for setting people free rather than attributing the power to Satan is essential. The importance of knowing the difference between good and evil has been desirable since Eden. Some churches have taught that the gifts of the Spirit are not to be used now. How unusual it would be for God to send the Holy Spirit to continue the work of Christ (John 14–16) and then discontinue his work a few years later. That would leave us powerless and as orphans. If you are uncertain about these principles, be sure to read the books of John and Acts. Record your reactions.

The next gift has caused considerable controversy in modern church history. *Speaking in tongues* is "the special Spirit-given ability to speak in sounds and utterances previously unknown to the speaker" (p. 133). The flow and syntax of the language may be different from the speaker's usual language. Additionally, the hearers understand what is being said in their own language (Acts 2:5–11). (See the next gift.) In Acts 2:17–21, Peter explains that this phenomenon had been predicted in the Old Testament in Joel 2.

There are several streams of thought regarding the gift of speaking in tongues. One is that the gift of tongues is no longer appropriate. The other is that people who are not speaking in tongues cannot really be expressing themselves adequately in prayer. Each belief system has numerous qualifiers, so the gift can be used and misused in various ways.

My own belief is that tongues are as valid now as they were in the early church, just as all the gifts are currently valid gifts of the Holy Spirit. The Holy Spirit did not cease to exist when Christ returned to heaven. In fact, the Lord said he *must* leave so that the Holy Spirit could come (John 16). It is quite clear that after Jesus ascended back into heaven, the Holy Spirit was sent to carry on the work that Christ began. It is unfortunate that one gift has resulted in so much controversy in the body of Christ. A gift is sent from the giver to be used with joy by the recipient.

I have found that speaking in an unknown language is a form of exalted praise to God. I have used it in prayer on occasion when my native language, English, seemed inadequate. I did not understand the language I was using, but the words sounded the same each time I prayed in an unknown language. Work through your own thoughts regarding the gift of tongues. However, consider that the Holy Spirit has been given to carry on the work of Christ through his gifts.

Have you ever heard someone speak in a language foreign to the speaker? Have you been blessed by it? Did you understand it? If you did, it may have been given for your benefit.

Interpreting tongues is the last gift mentioned in this 1 Corinthians passage. It is defined as "the special Spirit-given ability to interpret into known language a message spoken in tongues" (p. 109). It is considered that speaking in an unknown language in a group setting is not valid unless someone present can interpret the message into the language of the group. This would not apply if you were using the unfamiliar language in private prayer or praise. There is no direct reference to someone using the interpretation of tongues, except that each one heard the words in their own language (Acts 2). That is a pretty profound interpretation.

The conflict surrounding speaking in an unfamiliar language applies, as well, to interpreting that language. I have heard someone speaking in an unknown language and then heard someone else interpret what was said. It can be very moving. The awareness of the presence and power of the Holy Spirit is very enriching.

Record your thoughts.

All these are gifts of the Holy Spirit. God has given people like you and me the ability to do supernatural things. *Supernatural* means "relating to an order of existence beyond the visible observable universe … relating to God."[16] Think for a moment. You can do things beyond your natural abilities through the power of the Holy Spirit, just because he loves you and wants you to minister in his name.

Other gifts listed in the New Testament are also significant. In addition, some gifts are not necessarily supernatural but have been used with great impact, such as administration, creativity, musical ability, and teaching. God has also appointed people in certain positions to help us grow in love and understanding. These include apostles, prophets, teachers, evangelists, shepherds, and administrators (1 Corinthians 12:28, Ephesians 4:11).

All the gifts are empowered by the same Holy Spirit (1 Corinthians 12:4). Summarize your thoughts on the gifts and how they are to be used so that you get the greatest meaning and flow from the preceding passages. Use the gifts God has given you for his glory. He chose them before you were born. Your joy will increase and the body of Christ will benefit. If you are not sure which gifts you have, there are several tests you can take in order to help you determine them. Many pastors will be able to give you guidance in recognizing your gifts and in learning how to use them.

---

[16]   *Merriam-Webster's Collegiate Dictionary*, 11th ed., s.v. "supernatural."

Integrating Theology and Psychology

Some think that theology and psychology are antagonistic. However, both disciplines can be practiced and woven together if you desire. *Theology* is the study of God, and includes his emotions and behavior. *Psychology* is the study of human (and animal) behavior and emotions. Since God became a man in the incarnation of Jesus, there can be much overlap if one chooses to look for it. A commitment to following God can change not only one's identity but one's behavior and eternal destiny as well.

The account of Saul, also known as Paul, in the New Testament is a primary example (Acts 9). Saul had a reputation as an ardent killer of Christians. He had been trained in a very strict sect of Judaism known as the Pharisees. He was a perfectionist in his commitment to what he believed to be the truth: that the Christ was polluting the pure teachings of the Old Testament. Following a dramatic conversion experience, his belief system changed completely. This resulted in dramatically changed behavior. He became a committed missionary, taking the gospel of Christ to many parts of the then-known world, including Europe. From there it was brought to America centuries later. You have heard the good news because of Paul. While his intense personality did not change, his identity and behavior were completely altered.

This can happen to you, whoever and wherever you are. If you have not accepted that Christ has given his life for you, let me invite you to be born again now. Let the Lord change your identity from that of a lost person to someone who is an adopted child of God, a part of his family. His gifts are all expressions of his love for you. Ask the Holy Spirit to be your guide in all things. You will be forever changed.

The Goal

The goal of this chapter has been to help you find your identity in Christ. In addition to living by the fruit of the Spirit and using the gifts of the Spirit, there are other ways to give glory to God. If you recognize *the centrality of God in all things,* you will be living a life that reflects his glory to those around you. He is the Creator and Sustainer of the universe, the center of all things. He is the purpose of all things. "For from him and through him and to him are all things" (Romans 11:36).

> For by him all things were created, in heaven and on earth, visible and invisible … all things were created through him and for him. And he is before all things and in him all things hold together.
> —Colossians 1:16–17

> For whom and by whom all things exist.
> —Hebrews 2:10

It is pretty clear that the universe and everything in it exists by, for, and through God. You get to participate in making that known to the whole world. God has given you the elements of your identity in order for you to participate in fulfilling his command: "Go therefore and make disciples of all nations" (Matthew 28:19). The culture has sought to reverse things, to make it seem that God, if you believe in him at all, is here for your convenience, rather than you being here to exalt him.

For an in-depth review of forces that have impacted the culture negatively, see Ross Douthat's *Bad Religion: How We Became a Nation of Heretics* (New York: Free Press, 2012). Having been a psychologist for many years, it is personally painful to acknowledge that psychology has been a contributing factor in the decline of a God-centered culture. Psalm 119:11 says, "I have stored up your word in my heart, that I might not sin against you." Internalizing the Word of God is the most powerful defense against the temptations that Satan is going to bring against you. Being empowered by the Holy Spirit is the only way to live the abundant life.

God Has Chosen You.

Part 2

What He Asks of Us

For we are his workmanship, created in Christ Jesus for good works, which God prepared beforehand, that we should walk in them.
—Ephesians 2:10

4

LOVING HIM

What is the greatest commandment?
I wanted to know.

The most important is this ... you shall love the Lord your God
with all your heart and with all your soul and with all your
mind and with all your strength.

—Mark 12:30

That is a lot of love. Your whole being is to be engaged in loving God.
No part of you is excluded from this command. Jesus called it the greatest
commandment. Since that was his choice for the greatest commandment,
you need to pay particular attention to it.

Merriam-Webster's defines *love* as a "strong affection for another
arising out of kinship or personal ties: warm attachment, enthusiasm or
devotion."[17] God commands us to have strong personal ties to him. Vine
further defines love as "a strong emotional attachment."[18]

Do you have a strong emotional attachment to God? If not, what is
holding you back?

---

[17] *Merriam-Webster's Collegiate Dictionary*, 11th ed., s.v. "love."

[18] *Vine's Concise Dictionary*, s.v. "love."

God is love (1 John 4:16). That is his very essence. John 3:16 states that "God so loved the world that he gave his only begotten son." Giving is one of the characteristics of love. It is also one of the outstanding characteristics of God.

Is love one of your major characteristics?

O'Collins and Farrugia have a slightly different definition of love. Love is "that free, self-transcending, life giving, and unifying approval that has its source and standard within the life of the blessed Trinity."[19] Two words catch my attention: *self-transcending* and *approval*. God approves of those he loves; he gives them his approval. And his love is self-transcending. He is the center of the universe, yet the focus of his love and attention is on you, his beloved. That is truly astounding!

Let those words roll around in your mind until you have internalized them. Make some notes about what it means to you.

Mark uses the Greek word for love: *agape*. The meaning includes esteem, affection, and loving action. It is based on emotions but moves into action-based commitment. Vine says, "Love can be known only from the actions it prompts."[20] It is self-transcending, as O'Collins and Farrugia have described.

Does this feel familiar based on what you have experienced as love?

How does your experience differ from loving actions?

---

19   O'Collins and Farrugia, *Concise Dictionary of Theology*, s.v. "love."

20   *Vine's Concise Dictionary*, s.v. "love."

Other components included in loving him are worshipping him (Psalms 29, 95; Luke 4:8; John 4), doing what he does (John 14), and giving him thanks (Psalms 30, 118). The most significant sign of love is that it gives. Loving God is not always easy, but it is always simple. It simply means putting God first in everything.

Do you enjoy worshipping him?

What part of the worship service do you enjoy most?

God says, *"You are my friends if you do what I command you"* (John 15:14, emphasis added).

How can God and others know that you love him? Do you keep his commandments? With which ones do you have the most difficulty?

How often do you do what he asks you to do?

Do you enjoy giving financially? How do you see this as part of worshipping God? Do you give cheerfully?

Do you see prayer as part of your worship of him?

Do you give him thanks and praise him in all things?

Loving God with All Your Heart

The most important love in life is love for God. Love for God will influence all other relationships. The heart is generally seen as the center of the emotional self. Whether the heart is thought of in biological terms as the organ for distributing blood and oxygen to the rest of the body or in spiritual or psychological terms as the origin of the emotions, it is generally accepted as the beginning point.

We rarely, if ever, speak of emotional pain originating in the brain or other organ of the body. We speak of a broken heart rather than a broken brain or lung. David was a man whose emotions ran deep. Read several of the psalms he wrote. Within these verses, you will find an emphasis on protection and provision. These are two primary components of the expression of love. The lover wants to protect and provide for the beloved. You are God's loved one. He asks that you make him your loved one. Think of him first in everything, put him first in all you do. Let your love for him be the guide of your life. Jesus says if you love me you will keep my commandments (John 15). Let obedience be the primary expression of your love for him.

Dig into your heart for some of the following answers. Surface answers are obvious. Go deeper than the surface. Let the presence of the Holy Spirit give you awareness.

How is God protecting you?

How are you protecting God?

How is he providing for you?

What love are you providing for God?

Loving God with All Your Soul

The *soul* is defined as the "immaterial essence," "a person's total self."[21] O'Collins and Farrugia define the soul as the "spiritual principle of human beings that survives death."[22] Vine puts forth many of its uses in the New Testament, including "the breath of life," the seat of personality, and the will.[23] The word *psyche* is the Greek word for soul. It is the root of the word *psychology*.

What does that mean? What is a person's total self?

What does that mean to you?

For my own purposes of understanding, I have looked at the soul as being part of the will. In a healthy situation, the will draws information from the emotions, mind, and body and then integrates them into a unified whole to make a decision. If any element of our being is left out of the decision-making process, our "total self" will not be represented. Another way of looking at the soul is as a point of complete surrender, as Jesus did in Gethsemane. All areas of his being were surrendered to the will of his Father.

Has there been a time in your life when you had to make a choice between complete surrender to God, partial surrender, or refusal to surrender?

Which did you choose?

Why?

21   *Merriam-Webster's Collegiate Dictionary*, 11th ed., s.v. "soul."

22   O'Collins and Farrugia, *Concise Dictionary of Theology*, s.v. "soul."

23   *Vine's Concise Dictionary*, s.v. "soul."

What does complete surrender mean to you?

What if you don't like the possible outcome?

In Gethsemane, Jesus obviously knew the outcome of his Father's request and asked whether he might be spared. He also knew he would not be spared (Matthew 26:39).

Would the significance of his choice make his asking you to do something more acceptable?

Remember Jesus was tempted in every way that you might be tempted (Hebrews 4:15–16). He will understand your hesitation to surrender completely. However, he will be with you through the entire process. He will never leave you or forsake you. *He loves you beyond anything you can possibly imagine.* He wants to bless you beyond anything you can possibly imagine.

I realize many of you have never been loved to that degree in the human realm. But God says he will love you with an everlasting love. Everlasting is a long time: lasting forever. His love will never ever end. I know that is almost beyond comprehension, especially if you have not been greatly loved in this life. But he says it. It has to be true. He cannot lie.

Try loving him back with your whole self. Keep trying to increase your love and trust. Become intentional. He will reward you.

Record some ways in which you can increase your love for the Lord.

Loving God with All Your Mind

In David's writings, you find someone who used his mind to express his love to and for God. With your mind, you understand and form purpose. In *It's All about Him*, I listed several passages that express this concept (Brittell 2014, 45). Be sure to look them up in your Bible and read the context in which they are written in the psalms.

- He inquires.
- He waits.
- He rests.
- He meditates.
- He remembers.

These are all mental activities. He does all these with his mind. The physical representation of the mind is the brain. The brain is the most important organ in the body. It is influenced by everything that appears before your senses. What you see, hear, taste, smell, or touch is recorded in the brain and remains there (barring disease). If any of the senses is dulled by anything, the brain cannot function in its appropriate way, the way in which God designed it.

When a person is purposely anesthetized, some portion of the brain is rendered incapable of functioning. Paul, in Ephesians 5:19, says not to be drunk with wine but to be filled with the Spirit. The brain cannot function accurately if it is *under the influence* of any drug, wine, or liquor.

David says he will not set anything that is worthless before his eyes (Psalm 101:3). The whole of Psalm 101 is a statement of David's integrity before the Lord: what he will not tolerate in his life. David was a man after God's own heart. Unless there is a disability, you are capable of controlling your thoughts as well as controlling that which comes before your eyes or other senses. You are to love God with your entire mind, including all your senses and all your thoughts. Second Corinthians 10:5 says you are to take your thoughts captive to Christ. He said to do it. *The Lord never gives a command that is impossible to keep.* Record your thoughts.

How and what do you practice in order to keep your mind on God? If you are having difficulty keeping your mind on him, try some of the exercises mentioned in chapter 2.

Try memorizing and internalizing Scripture. It may not be the easiest thing in the world, but it can be very simple. Blocking out all other thoughts can be a challenge but is very rewarding. Jesus blocked out all other things except his love for his Father and you. He expressed this so well in John 17.

Loving God with All Your Strength

Loving God with all your strength means the strength of your entire body: heart, lungs, muscles, brain, bones, and everything that makes you strong, including what you eat.

Do you eat God-honoring food? Daniel was very clear that he and his friends did not want to eat the food provided by the king because it was too rich. He asked for and was given vegetables and water. God honored his choice (Daniel 1:8–21). One time when I was working on a very difficult situation with a patient, I went on a diet of water and vegetables and found it very helpful.

We don't know precisely what the disciples ate, but we do know they ate fish and bread. We also know that eating according to the law was part of their lifestyle. Daniel, Peter, and Paul are good examples of men who loved God with all their strength. The Christ is the perfect example.

After the resurrection, Peter and Paul as well as the other disciples devoted their entire beings (selves) to loving God and living to give him glory. Most of them endured tortured deaths. The Christ lived his whole life loving his Father.

As mentioned in *It's All about Him*, several giants of the faith in the Old Testament loved God with their entire strength (Brittell 2014, 46–47). It appears that, as humans, we need some time to mature enough to devote our entire body to loving God. By his grace, God appears to deal with us from a developmental perspective. He starts with the simple things and moves us to more complicated acts of devotion and obedience as we mature.

In *It's All about Him*, I cited Billy Graham and Jim Elliot as men who loved God with all their strength (Brittell 2014, 47). There is another, perhaps less famous, man who gave his strength to proclaiming his love for God. Eric Liddell, one of those on whom the movie *Chariots of Fire* was based, said, "God made me fast. When I run I feel his pleasure."[24] He refused to run on Sundays. This caused quite a stir within the Olympic community, but he held fast to his principles. He loved God with all his strength, mind, soul, and heart. He used his strength to bring glory to God. God rewarded him in return. You will never out-love God.

You, too, can use your strength to love God even though you may not have the kind of strength or fame as those I've mentioned. However, you are commanded to love God with all your strength, no matter what that level is. There may be times in your life when you can do unusual things for the glory of God, things you did not believe you could accomplish. Learning to recognize the voice of the Holy Spirit will enable you to do more than you ever thought possible as you move in obedience to his voice.

In my own life, I felt stunned when God opened the door for me to go to graduate school to become a PhD in psychology. I came from humble beginnings and never imagined that I could accomplish such a feat, or that I would practice professionally for several decades. My first job was chopping cotton on my father's farm. My model for a prayer of gratitude was David's prayer in 2 Samuel 7:18–29, expressing his gratitude that God took him from following the sheep in his father's pasture to becoming king of Israel (2 Samuel 7:8). David was further awed that God was going to build a house for him rather than the other way around. God uses whatever he has given you as long as you are surrendered to him.

What are your physical strengths?

---

[24] Hugh Hudson, David Puttnam, Colin Welland, Nicholas Farrell, Nigel Havers, Ian Charleson, Ben Cross, et al, 2005. *Chariots of Fire*. Burbank, CA: Warner Home Video.

How do you use them for the glory of God?

Love Is …

First Corinthians 13:4–8 defines love.

> Love is patient, love is kind and is not jealous; love does not brag and is not arrogant or rude. It does not insist on its own way; it is not irritable or resentful; it does not rejoice at wrongdoing, but rejoices with the truth. Love bears all things, believes all things, hopes all things, and endures all things. Love never ends.

I defined the words in *It's All about Him* (Brittell 2014, 50–58).[25] The definitions will not be repeated wholly here; however, one or two lines from each will be repeated.

Love Is Patient

Patience means bearing or enduring pain, trouble … without complaining or losing self-control … calmly tolerating delay, confusion or inefficiency.

Patience is a fruit of the Holy Spirit. "How skilled are you at allowing the Holy Spirit to control your thoughts, emotions and behavior" (Brittell 2014, 48)?

Spend some time meditating on what it means to be patient. Pray and ask the Holy Spirit to show you areas in which you need to increase your patience. Practice using new ways of thinking about events or ideas to help you develop new skills. Record them so you can follow up on them.

---

[25] All definitions in this section are taken from *Webster's New World Dictionary*, 2nd ed. (Simon & Schuster, New York, NY, 1986).

Love Is Kind

To be *kind* means to be sympathetic, friendly, gentle, and affectionate. Kindness is also a fruit of the Holy Spirit. To the degree that kindness is obvious in your life, your submission to the Holy Spirit is causing the fruit of kindness to emerge. What a wonderful combination.

To whom are you kind?

To whom and in what circumstance do you find it difficult to be kind?

What reaction emerges instead of kindness? Be honest with yourself and God in answering these questions.

Love Does Not Envy

To *envy* is to be discontented or have feelings of ill will because of another's advantage.

Have you at some time been foolish, led astray, a slave to your feelings, passing your days in malice and envy, hating and being hated by others (Titus 3:3)? What an incredible waste of time. How dishonoring to God, basically telling him he isn't running the universe according to your preconceived notions and desires. There seems to be a heavy dose of arrogance in there as well.

Several examples in *It's All about Him* may help you figure out your own envies (Brittell 2014, 50). Spend some time on this one. It can be ugly anywhere but especially in the body of Christ.

Make a list of times and people whom you have envied. Be ruthless with yourself, as this can be very subtle. It can be easy for you to deny your envy.

Love Does Not Boast

To *boast* means to talk about your accomplishments and about yourselves, showing too much pride and satisfaction. David, Jeremiah, and Paul say our boasting is to be in the Lord. (See *It's All about Him* for references [Brittell 2014, 50–51].)

Since everyone is gifted in some way, everyone is vulnerable to falling into this trap. False humility, the opposite of boasting, can be an equally dangerous trap. Review your interactions with others.

In what ways do you boast about any talent or ability you may have?

How do you consciously practice humility?

How does Satan get you to boast, and about what?

How do you resist self-aggrandizement?

Love Is Not Arrogant

Arrogance means to have overbearing pride or self-importance: thinking you are better than you are. I used to think arrogance meant to think you were better than someone else. However, when I looked it up in the dictionary, I discovered it meant that you think you are better than you are. It is not a comparative assessment in reference to someone else. It is all about you. How sad to have an inflated opinion of yourself.

Be sure to look at the questions in *It's All about Him*, especially the passage in 2 Corinthians 10:12 (Brittell 2014, 51–52). Attempting to compare yourself with someone else shows that you are not understanding the issue. No two people have the exact same gift to the exact same degree. You need to understand that it is God who gives all good gifts. Since you are the recipient of the gifts, you need an attitude of humility and praise.

How often do you try to take credit for something God has initiated?

Love Is Not Rude

To be *rude* is to be crude, uncouth, and discourteous.

Who needs a Christian who is rude or uncouth to God or others? "Let no corrupting talk come out of your mouth … and do not grieve the Holy Spirit of God, by whom you were sealed" (Ephesians 4:29–30). Other passages include Colossians 3:8–9 and Colossians 4:6. I am reminded of the rudeness of the Pharisees to the Christ.

The following are questions to provoke your thinking:

How rude are you to God on a scale of 1–10?

How often do you ask him to watch TV or play games with you?

Remember your body is the temple of the Holy Spirit, so everywhere you go, he goes. He has to be there with you in all the things you are doing.

How often do you listen for his voice before you take part in something?

When do you let his conviction move you to a different perspective?

Love Does Not Insist on Its Own Way

Insisting on one's own way is the expression of total self-centeredness.

How is God to be glorified if it is all about you?

"But for those who are self-seeking and do not obey the truth, but obey unrighteousness, there will be wrath and fury," said God through Paul (Romans 2:8). I didn't say it; he did.

This brings you back to the concept of the soul, the will.

My right is to go to hell because of the condition of my birth, born in trespasses and sin (Ephesians 2:5). Everything else is a gift from God by his grace.

Whose wishes are to be followed: God's or yours?

Christ demonstrated the totality of submission: thy will be done.

How do you try to impose your will on a situation?

To what do you feel entitled?

Are you trying to create a way to eternal life other than the one provided by Christ?

Love Is Not Irritable

To be *irritable* is to be easily annoyed or impatient.

The book of Proverbs says, "A soft answer turns away wrath … A hot-tempered man stirs up strife" (Proverbs 15:1, 18). "Whoever is slow to anger is better than the mighty, and he who rules his spirit than he who takes a city" (Proverbs 16:32). You can see more clearly how ugly irritability is when you think of the beauty of patience in contrast. God is so patient with us.

Take time to think of how longsuffering and patient the Lord is.

How often do you have to learn the same lesson over and over again, thinking this time you have finally understood and learned the lesson?

Write down some of your repetitious sins. We all have them.

Do you become irritable with people in your life who don't always get it right according to your perceptions? Describe your reactions.

Love Is Not Resentful

To be *resentful* is to feel bitterness or indignation from a sense of being offended.

Who hasn't felt offended or hurt over some perceived slight? Hebrews 12:15 says that you are to "see to it … that no 'root of bitterness' springs up in our lives." The only way to avoid resentment and bitterness is to practice daily forgiveness. A sense of offence may arise on a frequent basis. Given that life is "rough and tumble," it is likely that it will happen, at least occasionally. The only way to have victory over resentment is to practice forgiveness.

Forgiveness means to give up resentment. A lengthier explanation of what forgiveness requires and looks like is given in *It's All about Him* (Brittell 2014, 53–54). Basically, there are three important components:

- Recognize that sin has been committed against you.
- Recognize that you could let it overwhelm you and possibly ruin your life, or that you will make the choice to forgive the offender.
- Ask the Lord to glorify himself through the situation.

Forgiveness may be necessary several—or even many—times for the same offense. Some offenses keep coming back into memory and need to be forgiven each time they come back.

Think of times when you have chosen to forgive rather than holding a grudge or planting a seed of bitterness. Record these for future reference.

Who do you need to forgive and for what?

Love Does Not Rejoice at Wrongdoing

Wrongdoing is not in accordance with God's desire or design for humanity.

The works of the flesh, the weaker element in the nature of man, are found in Galatians 5:19–21 as well as other passages (Brittell 2014, 55). They all fall under the category of wrongdoing. There may be others unique to you. They are all sin.

As you read through all the passages, make note of those that tempt you the most. Everyone has vulnerabilities. Often, certain types of sin appear to run in families. Whether this is the result of genetic predisposition or familial modeling, psychology has not been able to discern with certainty. However, God calls it sin, and Jesus died to give you the victory over it, whatever the cause.

Make a list of those sins you recognize as tempting for you. Be ruthless with yourself so that God doesn't have to be more stern than gracious in dealing with you.

Be careful not to ask someone else to join you in wrongdoing. That would bring great displeasure from the Lord. (See 2 Samuel 11.)

Praise the Holy Spirit for the gift of conviction. He is calling attention to things that need to be confessed, repented of, and stopped. The forgiveness of God is the most powerful cleansing process in life and leads to unspeakable joy.

Love Rejoices with the Truth

To *rejoice* means to be happy, glad, and full of joy. *Truth* means to be in accordance with the facts.

You are to be full of joy whenever truth occurs, whether as a result of something you have chosen or from someone else's choice. Jesus is *the* truth and the Holy Spirit is *the* Spirit of truth. He lives within each born-again person. He is given to you as the seal of your salvation. When you are born again, your body becomes a temple of the Holy Spirit. You could say you are to be a temple of truth.

In some parts of today's world, truth has taken on a relative aspect. Your truth may be presented in such a way that it appears to be a personal truth, that it may not have the same meaning as my truth. You may want to go back to the meaning given in the dictionary. Truth is in accordance to the facts. Facts rarely change, although in today's world of relativism, an attempt to change the facts or reinterpret them is not uncommon. But why be sorry when you can be safe?

"Grace and truth came through Jesus Christ" (John 1:14). "The truth will set you free" (John 8:32). Who doesn't want to be set free from something, either from your own sin or fear or from having been sinned against by someone else? Even the Christ was mightily sinned against. He was ultimately set free from his body of death. He was transported back to the heaven from which he had come.

Are you fanatical about the truth?

Would that all were! The martyrs, past and present, are willing to die rather than deny the truth.

Do you adhere to the truth in all the venues of your life? Give examples.

In which areas do you find it most difficult to be committed to truth?

Do a word study on truth. Pledge yourself to being a person of truth. Even calling the Pharisees snakes and vipers was an act of truth.

Truth is truth. You are to rejoice whenever it emerges, whatever the context or occasion. Do you rejoice at the truth, or do you believe in shades of gray when it comes to truth?

To whom do you model truth?

Love Bears All Things

To *bear* is to carry, sustain, or support.

Many of the psalms, as well as other passages, reflect on the sustaining power of God in our lives. "The Lord is my rock and my fortress and my deliverer, my God, my rock, in whom I take refuge, my shield, and the horn of my salvation, my stronghold" (Psalm 18:2). That verse puts it all in perspective: he is all the strength and protection I need.

Our worship hymns often speak of his sustaining power. *It's All about Him* lists several of the many verses that speak of God being our shelter, rock, hiding place, strength, and fortress (Brittell 2014, 55).

List ways that you can express love by being strong and supportive.

Do word studies on some of the descriptors of carrying and being supportive, such as being our rock, shelter, and hiding place, that are most meaningful to you. Record the passages so you can go back to them as needed.

What did you learn from the word studies?

Can you feel the safety of being in God? If not, explore why you are anxious or fearful rather than realizing he is your support.

To whom do you model these qualities? Do you point the way to the ultimate protector when you are interacting with others?

Do you seek to protect others from engaging in sin? Give an example.

Ephesians 5 speaks of the husband being a protector for his wife even as Christ protects us, his chosen ones. As a husband, are you a protector? If not, from whom do you need to seek help?

Protection is a clear sign of love.

Love Believes All Things

To *believe* is to accept as true or real. It is to trust or have confidence in.

Throughout scripture, you are instructed to trust God. Love says God is trustworthy. You can believe him in all things. In my own life, I found trusting God to be very pleasant as long as I was living in close contact with him. It became more difficult when I began to detach emotionally. Even the giant of the faith, Abraham, who is known for his faith in God, did not always hold firmly to trust. The result for Abraham, or David, or any of the stalwarts of the faith, was the same as it is for you and me when we don't trust God: sin.

God has given you all things to enjoy: life, breath, beauty, comfort, himself, friendships, food, drink, health, rest, transportation, more beauty, and always more of himself. The universe functions in a predicable way. He always keeps his word. If he has promised disaster for disobedience, disaster occurs. If he has promised reward for obedience, reward happens. He has promised to love you forever. He does so, even when he is angry.

How can you not believe him and trust him?

Believing is not an emotion. It is a choice based on truth and on what you know of God's history. He has never been, nor can he ever be, untrustworthy. He will never go back on his promises.

Do word studies on believing God. I think you will be surprised at how your own awareness changes as you become more familiar with the history of God's love and faithfulness to his chosen ones.

Redirect your belief system so that it is directed toward trusting God. Believing or trusting others will often lead to disappointment and sometimes to depression. When man's breath departs, "he returns to the earth; on that very day his plans perish" (Psalm 146:4). We are still made of dust.

Record changes in your belief system as you go through the Scriptures.

Love Hopes All Things

Hope is the desire that what you want to happen will happen.

Again, the hope must be placed in God, not in man. "Hope in God; for I shall again praise him, my salvation, and my God" (Psalm 42:5). "Character produces hope, and hope does not put us to shame, because God's love has been poured into our hearts through the Holy Spirit who has been given to us" (Romans 5:5).

God himself says you are to hope in him. When you think of the enormity of who he is, hoping in him is logical as well as a profound privilege. Also, listen to the other part: God's love has been poured into your heart.

Do you know why he chose to pour his love into your heart?

Who can answer that? It is one of the mysteries of God that he chose those whom he did. Job 13:15, Psalm 39:7 and Romans 5:4–5 demonstrate how Job, David and Paul put their hope in God. You can share with others that he is the source of all hope.

Make a list of times when you have given up hope in God, times when you felt he simply did not care and had no interest in rescuing you from whatever the situation might be. Do some introspection to determine what caused your faith to crumble.

Then find a passage that declares that there is always hope in God.

Lois Brittell, PhD

Love Endures All Things

To *endure* is to hold up under, or bear, or put up with. It is somewhat similar to *bearing*, seen earlier in the chapter.

"The one who endures to the end will be saved" (Matthew 24:13). When Jesus is speaking to the seven churches in Revelation 2 and 3, he speaks of enduring to the end and the rewards that will accompany that endurance. Jesus endured the suffering on the cross for you. He says that if you love him, you will endure whatever God brings into your life.

God promises great reward for endurance. Hebrews 10:35–12:11 speaks of endurance that continues to eternal life. The writer of Hebrews says that you need to endure so that when you have done the will of God you may receive what is promised. Always, there is a promise of reward for faithful endurance. The Hebrews passage, although long, gives a detailed account of those in history who were rewarded. The reward is exemplary: that you may share his holiness and the peaceful fruit of righteousness (Hebrews 12:10–11). He is always faithful.

What are you enduring now?

Name some things you have endured in the past.

Have you received your rewards or are the rewards in the future?

Another word for endurance is *perseverance*. In Romans 5, Paul says that suffering produces perseverance that will produce character and hope. I addressed the relationship between bearing all things and hope in an earlier section. First Peter 2 says that it is a gracious thing, when mindful of God, to endure unjust suffering.

Numerous passages refer to endurance or perseverance. Looking them up in your concordance will help you understand what endurance means and how to do it. It is possible that in your lifetime you may be asked to endure suffering for the sake of Christ. Many Christians throughout the world are being commanded to renounce their faith or endure terrible suffering. Persecution may spread into our country and into your life.

Write down your reactions to the idea of suffering for the sake of Christ and the gospel.

Is your love for God so great that you are preparing yourself spiritually to endure all things for his sake?

How are you training yourself to endure in the smaller issues of life, such as enduring a hostile family member, neighbor, or mate?

Love Never Ends

End means to stop or to cease to exist.

God says love never stops or ceases to exist. His love never stops or ceases to exist.

What does that mean? Can you even absorb the concept? If you answered the questions in *It's All about Him*, you will have a sense of the everlasting quality of God's love (Brittell 2014, 58).

At the beginning of this section I quoted from 1 Corinthians 13:4–7. I would like to end this chapter with another passage from 1 Corinthians 13:1–3.

> If I speak in the tongues of men and of angels, but have not love, I am a noisy gong or a clanging cymbal. And if I have prophetic powers, and understand all mysteries and all knowledge, and if I have all faith, so as to remove mountains, but have not love, I am nothing. If I give away all I have, and if I deliver up my body to be burned, but have not love, I gain nothing.

The Goal

The goal of this chapter has been to help you understand, express, and experience love in a brand-new way. In our culture, people talk a great deal about love. Some of their talk is valid; much is not. The Bible gives us examples and experiences of love in a way that nothing else can. God is love. Without God, there is no real love.

God Is Love

5

Love Your Neighbor as Yourself: In Him

Who is my neighbor?
I wanted to know.

The second [commandment] is this, "You shall
love your neighbor as yourself."
—Mark 12:31

Characteristics of Love

This commandment, the second one, is part of the greatest commandment Christ gave. It includes the first commandment, emphasized in the preceding chapter. "There is no other commandment greater than these" (Mark 12:31).

This commandment can apply to anyone other than God. It represents the crossbar on the cross, Christ reaching out his hands to encompass the whole world in giving his life. Whoever wishes to be enfolded by those arms can be loved by the living God. All you have to do is repent, believe in him, and accept his free gift of salvation as the Holy Spirit gives you grace to do these things.

"By this all people will know that you are my disciples, if you have love for one another" (John 13:35, emphasis added).

I will emphasize the meaning of love again in this chapter. It bears repeating in order to be able to really internalize what it means to love and be loved. Today's culture exhibits so many false expressions of love. Sentimentality, manipulation, control, and infatuation are not love. *Ahab,* the Greek word used for love in this passage, is defined by Vine as "a strong emotional attachment to and desire either to possess or to be in the presence of the object: familial, romantic or friendship."[26] *Ahabah,* the noun form, can be used to refer to "family, friend, romantic or sexual love."

I have found that "being in the presence of," reflects my own emotional desire. It would be interesting to do a survey to see which of the two expressions of love are the most frequent: whether the "possessive" part or "being in the presence of" would be the most significant.

In love from God, I want to be "possessed" by God as well as being in His presence. In friendship, I want to be in my friends' presence.

Which desire do you most prefer? Are the differing preferences dependent on the lover?

God is love, and love is of God. The most profound basis for relationship is love. God created it as an expression of himself. It is also an expression to be shared between two people as in romantic or marital love. In the case of familial love or friendships, it may exist between however many are involved in the intimacy of that relationship. O'Collins and Farrugia describe love as "that free, self-transcending, life-giving, and unifying approval that has its source and standard within the life of the blessed Trinity and that justifies saying 'God is Love.'"[27] Read that several times. When you get it, it is a profound statement. However, it may take several readings to absorb.

---

[26]   *Vine's Concise Dictionary,* s.v. "ahab."

[27]   O'Collins and Farrugia, *Concise Dictionary of Theology,* s.v. "love."

I have found three components that seem to be present consistently on the part of the lover toward the beloved. They are the desire to give to, the desire to protect, and the desire to provide for.

As you read through and work on the rest of the chapter, see whether you can consistently find these three elements in the relationships being studied. See if at least one of them is there in each scenario, and if so, which one?

You have looked at definitions from reliable resources. Now lets look at how it feels.

How does it feel to love or be loved?

How does it feel to want to be in the presence of the loved one, often or constantly?

How does it feel to want to possess the beloved? Since this is your record, put into your words how it feels to you.

Are the two approaches to expressing love different for the different genders? Ask someone of the opposite gender.

Do you want to possess someone, do you want to be possessed by someone, or do you want to be in the presence of a particular person?

Are there any differences in how you and your loved one express feelings of love?

Look at your different loves, if there has been more than one. Write something about how you felt with each of them: lovers, mates, children, or friends. Were the longings of your heart the same in each circumstance?

Love in Friendship

One of the primary examples of love in the Bible was the friendship between David and Jonathan. In 1 Samuel 18:1–31, the writer says that Jonathan loved David "as his own soul" … "his soul was knit to the soul of David." Their love was, perhaps, as intense a love between any two people as was humanly possible, with the exception of the love Jesus had for his friends. Jonathan loved David so much that he gave up his right to the throne of his father, King Saul, so that David would become king.

All three expressions of love are evident in their relationship. Jonathan *protected* David from the rage of Saul. For his efforts, his father threw a spear at him. Certainly he *gave* to David when he gave him his princely equipment and stepped aside so that David could be king (1 Samuel 18:4). He *provided* a way of escape when Saul determined to kill David (1 Samuel 20).

When Jonathan died, David lamented greatly and said that he experienced Jonathan's love as greater than "the love of women" (2 Samuel 1:19–27). David had many wives and concubines. He would have had abundant opportunities for many expressions of love as well as plenty of sexual expression. However, he found Jonathan's love to be greater than them all.

"The soul of Jonathan was knit to the soul of David" (1 Samuel 18:1). Who did the knitting?

Have you loved anyone as your own soul? How does it feel for you? Was it reciprocated?

I have the privilege of belonging to a group of women whose friendship began in high school. We continue as friends today. We have served the Lord in various capacities from teaching to clinical psychology. We have supported each other through various life circumstances and continue to do so through the changes that are currently taking place, including the deaths of some of our husbands.

In addition to women friends, I have had friendships with men. What is different with friendships with men is the need to maintain good boundaries so that sexuality does not enter into the relationship. In true friendship, that boundary is equally important to all the participants. What was the same was the desire to give to, to provide for, and to protect the relationship. I don't recall wanting to be possessive. In friendship, exclusivity was not an expectation.

A person may have several friends of either gender at the same time. Love in friendship is a profound gift, whether that friendship is with same-sex friends or friends of the opposite gender. Friendship is an expression of loving your neighbor as yourself. It fulfills Jesus's admonition to let others know you are his disciples by your love.

Have you had one or more close friendships that you enjoyed?

Describe what you contributed to the friendship?

In the case of Christ and his disciples, John is described as "the disciple whom Jesus loved" (John 21:20). Peter, James, and John were chosen to go up to the Mount of Transfiguration with Jesus (Matthew 17:1–2). Even among Jesus's friendships, there were different degrees of intimacy. Clearly, Jesus loves you as much as he loved himself. His one desire was to do the will of his Father. That is his desire for you, as well. He lived, died, and rose again so that you might be empowered to do the will of the Father in your own life. You are his friend if you do what he commands. His command was that we love one another as he loved us (John 15:12–14). Love in friendship can be lifesaving.

Record your thoughts.

Another kind of love mentioned in the Bible suggests a deeper, more profound form of relationship.

Love in Marriage

In *It's All about Him*, I presented several different situations in the Bible in which love was expressed in such a way that it could qualify for loving your neighbor as yourself (Brittell 2014, 67–70). There were differing courtships, differing kinds of marriages, even differing kinds of love for different children. Marriage to more than one wife often created tension when the husband loved the childless wife more than the wife who bore him children. I was deeply touched by the love Elkanah expressed for his wife, Hannah, who was barren. "Am I not more to you than ten sons?" (1 Samuel 1:8)

How does a woman answer that?

Have you loved someone with the intensity Elkanah expressed?

In two marriages, we saw husbands who clearly loved one wife more than they loved the other. Jacob, married to Rachel, and Elkanah, married to Hannah, loved their barren wives more than they loved the wives who bore their children.

Which marriage could you relate to most? Did you bear children, or not?

In the New Testament, Ephesians 5:22–33 speaks clearly of the love the husband is to have for his wife, modeled on the love Christ has for us, his church-bride. I hope if you are a wife, as you read the biblical text, you will take very seriously the imperative to respect, honor, and submit to your husband. The current social emphasis on equality in all things between the husband and wife is not biblically supported. In God's sight, we are all equal, but our roles within marriage are different.

The husband's responsibility to be the protector, provider, and lover is so large that every man needs the empowerment of the Holy Spirit to do this adequately. Men need Christ to be the role model. Husbands are assigned as much greater responsibility for loving their wives as greater responsibility is assigned to Christ in his love for us.

Christ's submission on our behalf occurred on the cross in submission to his Father. Some have interpreted Ephesians 5:21 to be part of the marriage instruction. In the Greek, that verse is part of the "one-another" instructions in the preceding passage. Nowhere is Christ instructed to submit to us, his church-bride. He fulfilled his part in giving his life for us at Calvary. For us, the bride of Christ, it is imperative that we submit to his lordship. It is essential that the husband love his wife as Christ loves his bride. It is essential that the wife show honor, respect, and submission to her husband. In today's world of abuse and cultural distortion, this passage requires special thought, prayer, and perhaps, counsel.

Husband, how are you giving your life for your wife? Holding down a job is not a sufficient fulfillment of this command. You are required by God to work, whether married or single (Genesis 2:15). If you don't work, you shouldn't eat (2 Thessalonians 3:10).

In today's culture, making the job the priority often causes and results from a lack of intimacy at home. Often emotional fulfillment occurs at the workplace rather than in the home. Sometimes sexual fulfillment follows. This destroys everything God had intended for the marriage.

Fidelity would be a good place to begin. Today one can scarcely leave home without being bombarded by temptation to be unfaithful in marriage. In the home, TV, computers, and publications all present temptations to infidelity. In the Old Testament, God's wrath was evident many times because of Israel's infidelity to him. The Israelites worshipped idols under every green tree. God's anger was so intense that he sent them into captivity in Babylon.

Is it clear to your wife that what you are doing is in fulfillment of this command, that your actions are an expression of your faith and love for both God and your wife? It may be especially difficult if she is not showing you the respect God commands.

Wife, are you showing honor and respect to your husband? God commands you to honor and respect your husband, not because of the way your husband treats you but because obeying God is his will. It may be difficult if your spouse does not love you as Christ loved his bride. It is still a command of God.

It may be difficult to fulfill your roles if your spouse is not fulfilling theirs. However, God will reward you. Pray for grace to be obedient to the Lord.

Record your thoughts.

As a psychologist specializing in marital problems, I saw a severe breakdown in the fulfillment of both parts of God's command for marriage. However, I also saw great reward for those who fulfilled their part of the command regardless of whether their partner was fulfilling theirs (barring physical abuse).

In recent years, I have observed several couples committed to exclusivity (betrothed), although they did not marry. According to 1 Corinthians 7:36–38, this is an acceptable form of love in which it is the man's responsibility to make the choice not to be sexually active, "having his desire under control." In the couples I have observed, the commitment to each other is firm. This would seem to be a very deep form of friendship. As Paul acknowledged, this is his opinion, not the directive of the Lord.

Sexual Love

The Song of Solomon is the clearest biblical example of feelings that accompany sexual loving and being loved. The story is about two people of the opposite gender who are very expressive in their declarations of love. There have been many interpretations of the meaning of this book. (See *It's All about Him* [Brittell 2014, 70].) I prefer to take the Song of Solomon at face value—as the story of biblical sexual love. Read the whole book together with your mate. Since love and sexual expression of it are gifts from God, accept it as written and learn from God how to be good lovers.

One of the most notable expressions of love is the attribution of perfection described throughout the book by both the lover and the beloved (chapters 4–6).

Have you felt or do you feel passionate about someone?

Do you tell your beloved how beautiful he or she is? Are your words well received?

Have you felt that the one you loved was perfect in any or every way? How did you express your feelings?

Although the psalms are full of emotional expression, sexuality was not included in the passion expressed there. The Song of Solomon is the only book that is devoted specifically to addressing sexual love. It is beautiful and detailed in its content. You can learn from it how to be a good lover. Proverbs 5 also addresses how to be a good lover.

How do you feel about these passages?

What Happens if You Are the Unloved Person in the Relationship?

In many of the relationships presented earlier in the chapter, there was a person who was loved, and that love was expressed. However, in several biblical stories, there was a person who was not loved but was rejected.

How did they manage their rejection?

Let's look at the first one. God accepted Abel's offering but rejected Cain's without explaining why (Genesis 4). Theologians offer several explanations for why Cain's might have been rejected. But God doesn't tell us. The Lord placed a curse on Cain (Genesis 4:11). This is the first reference to a person being cursed. The serpent and the ground were cursed in the fall, but Adam and Eve were punished, not cursed. Cain's anger at God is clearly expressed in the conversation between Cain and God (Genesis 4:6–15). Cain, anguished, says, "My punishment is greater than I can bear" (Genesis 4:13). Being rejected is a humiliation at all levels, even though the Lord put a mark on Cain to protect him. "Then Cain went away from the presence of the Lord" (Genesis 4:16). Rejection is painful.

What would you have done if God had made it clear that he was rejecting you? How would you have responded?

Many generations later we find the story of Hagar and Ishmael (Genesis 16–17). Hagar was the servant of Sarai, Abram's wife. Sarai had been unable to conceive, so she told her husband to have intercourse with her servant, Hagar, which he did. Hagar conceived and gave birth to a son. After Ishmael's birth, Sarah (whose name was changed by God) demanded that Hagar and her son be thrown out of the home.

There were complications along the way, but eventually Hagar and Ishmael were thrown out. The Lord intervened and saved Ishmael's life when Ishmael was near death in the desert without water. The Lord said that Ishmael would "be a wild donkey of a man, his hand against everyone and everyone's hand against him, and he shall dwell over against his kinsman"(Genesis 16:12). Later, the Lord said to Abraham (whose name God also changed) that he would bless Ishmael and make him the father of twelve princes and "into a great nation" (Genesis 17:20). The difference between God's choice to honor Isaac, the son of promise, and Ishmael, the son of Sarah's impatience, is impressive. Again, you see that rejection causes a great deal of pain.

How would you—have you—expressed your pain at the rejection that was ordained by God?

In the next generation, there is another story of God's favoring one child over the other (Genesis 25:19–25). Rebekah bore twin sons to Isaac after he had prayed about his wife's barrenness. While the children were still in her womb, they were struggling. When she asked the Lord why this was happening, he told her that two nations were in her womb, and two peoples inside her. He said the one would be stronger than the other and the older would serve the younger.

As the boys grew up, Isaac loved Esau, while Rebekah loved Jacob. One day when Esau came in from hunting and was hungry, he sold his birthright and the blessing that went with it to Jacob for a pot of food. Jacob deceived his father and ended up getting the blessing that should have gone to the eldest son, Esau. "Esau lifted up his voice and wept" (Genesis 27:38). God had predicted which son would serve the other before either of them was born. While it was very painful for Esau, it was God's choice. In Malachi 1:2–6, the Lord again affirms his choice to love Jacob but to hate Esau. Since God is sovereign, his choice ultimately prevails.

God's choice in electing Israel to be his chosen people and the recipient of his blessings, as well as his great love for them, is clear throughout the Old Testament, particularly in Deuteronomy 7:7. God's choice to include the Gentiles in his plan of salvation in the New Testament is an indication of how great a gift salvation is to those who were not born Jews. You have the privilege of inheriting the blessings of God along with the Jewish people, totally as an act of his grace.

What are your feelings regarding God's rejection of whole peoples and his choice to bless another group?

A fourth example occurs in the life of Leah, Jacob's first wife. He had been promised Rachel and had worked for her hand for seven years. On the wedding night, their father, Laban, switched daughters. In the morning, Jacob found that he had had sex with the less attractive older daughter, Leah. After much negotiation, Jacob was able to have both wives. Rachel was the wife he loved, while Leah was the one he rejected, even though Jacob continued to "go in to her" (have sex with her). She continued to bear sons to Jacob. "When the Lord saw that Leah was hated, he opened her womb" (Genesis 29:31).

Leah understood that she was hated but kept hoping that her husband would become attached to her after she bore her third son. When that did not happen, after giving birth to her fourth son, she said, "This time I will praise the Lord" (Genesis 29:35). After the birth of her sixth son, she said, "God has endowed me with a good endowment; now my husband will honor me because I have borne him six sons" (Genesis 30:19). She was willing to settle for being honored rather than being loved. There is no indication that Jacob honored her. Leah turned to God for her consolation. He honored her. She is the mother of half of the twelve tribes of Israel, a magnificent honor. She appears to have handled her rejection with dignity, accepting God's will without rebellion.

Are you someone who has been rejected in love? How did you handle that?

Note that the two men mentioned, Cain and Esau, were both rejected by God. In the case of the two wives who were rejected by their husbands, Hagar and Leah, the Lord intervened on their behalf. The Lord promised to take care of widows. These two women were emotional widows, but the Lord blessed them.

Despite the possibility of rejection, the command is to love your neighbor as yourself. Within God's sovereign plan, rejection is possible and in some cases mandated. He still honors obedience.

Parental Love

Another love relationship manifest in Jacob's family is instructive for us. His favoritism for his son Joseph created all kinds of problems.

God has given instruction for raising our children. Children, too, fall under the mantle of loving your neighbor.

Have you loved all your children equally? Jacob clearly loved one of his children more than the others (Genesis 37). What is your reaction? Did the difference in degree of love create problems?

How have you refrained from provoking your children (Colossians 3:21)? Clearly, Jacob did not.

Loving your children is as much a command as any other. They are part of your neighborhood. God says the world will know you are a Christian by your love.

The Goal

The goal of this chapter has been to help you understand love in the interpersonal forms God has ordained and outlined in Scripture. Interpersonal love is commanded in the second commandment, which is part of the Great Commandment. Loving your neighbor, potentially all others except God, as yourself can be a genuine challenge. You must determine what it means to love yourself and whether or not you truly do. Loving oneself must not be confused with self-indulgence. You are asked to give of all that Christ has given you, not to be self-centered. You are asked to love in that self-transcending way that O'Collins and Farrugia describe as unifying approval, free, and life-giving.[28]

Love may originate in the mind, as in the case of friendship, where good boundaries may be needed, with the heart and soul following. When there may be less need for strong boundaries, as in marriage, love can originate in the heart, with soul, mind, and body following. Christ loved us from his heart, soul, mind, and body. He presents himself as our friend, lover, husband, and Savior.

Love is God's most precious gift. It results in giving life, whether in conceiving a child or in giving eternal life to those whom he has chosen. It resulted in Jesus giving his life. *Love always gives.*

Anyone But God Can Be Your Neighbor

---

[28] O'Collins and Farrugia, *Concise Dictionary of Theology*, s.v. "love."

6

PRAYING TO HIM: INTIMACY WITH GOD

How can I have intimacy with God?
I wanted to know.

I love you, O Lord, my strength. The Lord is my rock and my
fortress and my deliverer, my God, my rock, in whom I take
refuge, my shield, and the horn of my salvation, my stronghold.
I call upon the Lord, who is worthy to be praised, and I am
saved from my enemies.

—Psalm 18:1–3

How Do You Show Someone You Love Him or Her?

Communication is the most frequent way of expressing yourself
to another. Even in the animal kingdom, communication takes place
with sights, sounds, odors, and whatever form the Lord God put into
their system. Among human beings, talking is the most frequent form of
expression. Children try out their vocal cords to begin with and later turn
to babbling. Soon words and then sentences begin to emerge, usually to
the applause of those around them. They are learning to communicate.
Often, the first word they learn is *no*.

Communication is defined as "a process by which information is exchanged between individuals through a common system of symbols, signs or behavior."[29] The degree of communication between two people, given normal circumstances, may be an indicator of the level of intimacy that exists between them. If communication stops within a relationship, a serious breach may have occurred. Unless both parties have agreed not to communicate for a specific reason or season, loss of communication may indicate loss of affection by one or both parties. Communication is the conduit for relationship.

God initiated communication in the Garden of Eden. God thought it important to speak with the people created in his image. Unfortunately, Eve thought it of greater importance to speak with Satan. Take a moment to reflect on the significance of that one conversation followed by the consequences. Of course, you realize that it happened under the control of God's sovereignty.

One representative conversation had greater implications: when Jesus said, "I am the way, the truth and the life." (He said many things of equal significance about himself.) The point here is the significance of a single communication. One conversation can change the course of history for all time for every human being who has been or ever will be born.

Communication Is Important

We have no evidence that Adam or Eve prayed. People began to pray after the birth of Seth's son, Enosh, who was Adam and Eve's grandson. "At that time people began to call upon the name of the Lord" (Genesis 4:26). Seth was Adam and Eve's third son, early in the history of mankind. Many generations later, at the time they entered the land of Canaan some three thousand years ago, Moses told them, "But from there you will seek the Lord your God and you will find him, if you search after him with all your heart and with all your soul" (Deuteronomy 4:29). This promise says that you will find God if you search for him with all your heart and with all your soul, that is, earnestly. This was said to ordinary people, not just to the priests. From that time on, all people could seek and speak to the Lord God directly.

---

[29] *Merriam-Webster's Collegiate Dictionary*, 11th ed., s.v. "communication."

This form of communication with God is called prayer. *Prayer* is defined as "an address (as a petition) to God ... in word or thought: an earnest request or wish."[30] Vine defines prayer from the Greek as "a wanting, a need ... an asking, entreaty, supplication."[31] O'Collins and Farrugia say, "To pray is to invoke, adore, praise, thank, express sorrow, and ask blessings from our personal creator and Lord."[32] They suggest the psalms were the form of prayer in the Old Testament.

How have you enjoyed this great privilege?

We people communicate with each other fairly regularly. Communication in today's world can happen by several means unknown until the last few decades. Among them are texting, email, telephone, television, face book, Twitter, and various other forms of electronic communication. Our society has come to take these for granted. However, communicating with God seems to be more difficult than just pushing a button or clicking a key.

How do you touch a key earnestly?

Until Jesus came, it was uncommon for ordinary people to talk to God through ordinary conversation. The holy people did most of the praying and listening. The prophets often spoke to and listened to God. The Lord said that he spoke with Moses face-to-face as a man speaks to his friend. Moses was very direct in his communication with God. David often inquired of the Lord and spoke very directly to him. Other kings spoke to God directly or communicated through the prophets. In the New Testament, some two thousand years ago, ordinary people were taught how to speak to God in an ordinary way.

[30] *Merriam-Webster's Collegiate Dictionary*, 11th ed., s.v. "prayer."
[31] *Vine's Concise Dictionary*, s.v. "prayer."
[32] O'Collins and Farrugia, *Concise Dictionary of Theology*, s.v. "prayer."

Why Talk to God?

The question is often asked, "Doesn't God know what I need? Why do I have to pray?" Of course he does. Meditate on how much he desires to hear from you. If your children never spoke to you it would be considered abnormal. It is also abnormal not to talk to your heavenly Father.

Do you understand the incredible opportunity you have in being able to talk to the Creator of the universe and the Savior of your soul?

In the Old Testament, we begin to learn about prayer. In Genesis, Israel's blessings clearly were to come through Abraham and Sarah. That meant they had to have children. Abraham had talked with God about his lack of an heir. He even went so far as to impregnate Sarah's servant, Hagar, to produce an heir (Genesis 16). Abraham had tried to solve the problem on his own with Sarah's advice. You know how that worked out: their descendants are still at war with each other. Ishmael was not the son of promise. Their son, Isaac, was finally promised and born ten years later.

Rebekah, their daughter-in-law and Isaac's wife, was unable to conceive. This would have kept the promise from being fulfilled. When Rebekah's husband, Isaac, prayed that she might conceive, the Lord answered his prayer (Genesis 25:21).

Didn't the Lord know that Rebekah needed to conceive in order to fulfill his own promise? He is the one who ordained it.

How much did God value Isaac's humility and communication in asking for his help in making the promise come true? What do you think?

How often do you need to communicate with God? *It's All about Him* suggests topics for conversation with God (Brittell 2014, 81). One of the most frequent prayers might be prayer for forgiveness. Peter suggested seven times. Jesus said seventy times seven. That's 490 times (Matthew 18:21). Probably most of our needs are closer to Jesus's suggestion than to Peter's.

How often do you need to pray for forgiveness?

How often do you need to pray for comfort and hope?

How often do you need to pray to feel loved?

How often do you need to pray for strength?

We are commanded to pray without ceasing (1 Thessalonians 5:17). How impossible does it seem to be able to pray without ceasing?

The Bible and I suggest that prayer is something everyone can do. I recall the years I practiced as a psychologist. While conducting a session, I would suddenly realize I did not know how to answer an issue that the patient had just presented. Depending on the situation, I would send up an arrow prayer or stop and say, "I need to ask God what he wants us to do with this." The first time I did this, the patient would look surprised. Then, as the person realized I felt comfortable talking to the Lord in the middle of a session, they would tell me how they had begun to pray about more things.

Finding a time and place where you can concentrate will help you develop a vibrant prayer life so you can look forward to it.

Do you have a prayer chair or closet? It is worth your effort to establish one.

Some people have said they pray while driving the car or while they are in the shower. This is certainly multitasking. My concern is that one or the other activity, both of which are important, will not be getting full attention. Remembering that Jesus is the King of Kings might help you think of prayer as approaching the throne room. At this time in our culture, people have become very casual in their approach to things that used to be considered sacred. Praying while doing something else that doesn't require concentration may be better than not praying at all. I'm not sure. However, you also need time dedicated to having a concentrated conversation with the Lord. Remember he is the source of your life. He holds your breath in his hand. Everything that comes into your life has been ordained by or filtered through God.

Let us never forget that it is those who do not cherish sin in their hearts that can have their prayers answered (Psalm 66:18–20).

Examples of Prayer

The Lord's Prayer

Matthew 6:9–14 is the first conversation that Jesus taught people to have with God. It is variously called the Lord's Prayer or the disciple's prayer. The Lord's Prayer is a perfect model for beginning to learn to pray. Simple and straightforward, it expresses our most basic needs. Beginning with adoration appropriate for approaching the King (Matthew 6:9–10), it moves on to expressing our need for the day, "Give us this day our daily bread" (Matthew 6:11). The Lord, throughout the Bible, reminds us that he will supply our needs for the day, not for the week, month, or year.

Days are mentioned as the unit for creation. How many hours those days consisted of is not certain, but the Bible says, "There was evening and there was morning, the first day" (Genesis 1:5). God's emphasis has been on the day. The second clear example of this was the manna in the wilderness during the exodus (Exodus 16:31). The Israelites were to gather enough manna for one day. The Lord's Prayer again emphasizes the needs for the day. He wants us to understand and accept our dependence on him for meeting our needs daily.

Then Jesus focused on the need for both giving and receiving forgiveness (Matthew 6:12). Forgiveness is essential to our spiritual and psychological life. That, too, should be done daily. The need for protection and deliverance from evil: is there any protection that is more important than this? To be free from the influence of evil is crucial (Matthew 6:13). These are the things the Lord thought significant.

Do you think less of them? Which of these can you live without?

A Prayer of Repentance

It's All about Him presents two other prayers that are very close to my heart (Brittell 2014, 86–89). Daniel's prayer touched my heart when I was a young person. (See Daniel 9.) He was profoundly concerned about the sin of his nation. If the people of our nation would express the same concern for our country's sin, and would seek forgiveness with the same intensity Daniel expressed, talk show hosts would have something truly unusual to talk about. So would you as you saw the power of God at work in your culture. Let me encourage you to read the prayer often so that you internalize the anguish Daniel and God felt for the sin of his Holy City. Daniel expressed his anguish through prayer and humility.

How do you express your anguish for your country, city, family, or yourself?

How many sins does Daniel confess in his prayer? Let's look at a few examples.

- We have sinned.
- We have done wickedly.
- We have turned aside.
- We have not listened.
- We have rebelled.

Then Daniel asked the Lord to turn aside his anger, to make his face to shine on his sanctuary, and to forgive them (Daniel 9:17–19).

How often do you need to ask the Lord to turn his anger aside and make his face shine on you or your family or your country in blessing?

A Prayer of Love

The other prayer that touches my heart deeply is Jesus's prayer of intercession for his disciples and for us. (John 17). The intimacy and love expressed in his prayer are just short of overwhelming. Internalizing the love of the Father for the Son, the love of the Son for the Father, and the love of both of them for you and me is life changing. This prayer is so full of love there is scarcely room for any other concept. Following is my translation of some of the passages.

John 17

> It is time for me to come home, let me glorify you (v.1).
> You gave me all authority. I gave them eternal life (v.2).
> I glorified you by doing what you gave me to do (v.4).
> I taught those you had given me, about you (v.6).
> Please take care of those whom you have given me (v.9).
> I am coming home. They are still there (v.11).
> I am asking you to protect them from Satan (v.15).
> I am also asking for those who are going to believe in me (v.20).
> I ask that they may all be one in us (v.21).

Father, I desire that those you gave me might be with me (v.24).
[I ask] that the love with which you loved me may be in them
(v.26).

Record your thoughts.

"I am praying for them. I am not praying for the world but for those whom you have given me, for they are yours" (John 17:9). Christ is saying that you are the Father's gift to Jesus. Let the enormity of God's love pour over you and fill every crevice of your being. Read it often. "Greater love has no one than this, that someone lay down his life for his friends. You are my friends if you do what I command you" (John 15:13–14). Being a friend of Jesus is the highest possible calling in the universe. See *It's All about Him* for a more complete translation of chapter 17 (Brittell 2014, 88–89).

How much more could he have loved you than to give his life for you?

Do you thank him for it?

Prayer, the Sacrifice of Praise

Jeremiah, in Jeremiah 33:11, and Paul, in Romans 1:21, both speak of the importance of prayers of thanksgiving. Jeremiah refers to it as a sacrifice. When a person feels down and discouraged, praising God can feel like a sacrifice. Paul says the unrighteous did not honor God or thank him; instead, their hearts were darkened. They were not grateful enough to make the sacrifice of praise.

When David's son, conceived in sin, was near death, David prayed that his son might live (2 Samuel 12). If God had honored that prayer, he would have been rewarding sin. God said no, and the boy died. Then David went into the house of the Lord and worshipped. To praise God when he has said no to your request might be considered a sacrifice.

What feelings or memories do you have at this point?

David, a man after God's own heart, prayed one of the most beautiful prayers recorded in Scripture. Starting in humility, he moves on to adoration, and then to praise. His prayer touches my heart every time I read it. Read 2 Samuel 7:18–29.

He begins, "Who am I, O Lord God, and what is my house, that you have brought me thus far" (2 Samuel 7:18)? It reminds me of my own journey from chopping cotton on my father's farm to retiring as a clinical psychologist. Like David, I have praised God in amazement on numerous occasions.

What blessings had God given David?

How has God blessed you in extravagant ways? How have you praised him for them?

What has been your journey?

The psalms and the prophets record many requests for help. In the psalms, people prayed about every possible emotion. There is a request for vengeance in Psalm 94:1–7. How many times have you wanted to hurt someone who hurt you?

How many times have you asked God to do it for you? Did you pray Psalm 94?

Jesus often went up in a mountain to pray. He prayed for help three times in the garden of Gethsemane. Moses and David, two men who were very close to God's heart, prayed often for help.

Why do you think God honored them?

How does he show his great love for you through answered prayer?

Reflect on the many areas of your life in which you need help. When do you ask God to help you? How do you listen for his reply?

How do you praise him when he helps you?

Recording some of the areas in which you need help on a frequent basis, and noting some of the verses that address those needs, will help you develop intimacy with God.

Daniel offered a simple prayer of praise in Daniel 2:20–23. The Lord had spared his life and that of his three friends (Daniel 2:12) by telling Daniel Nebuchadnezzar's dream with its interpretation while they served the king in captivity.

Has your life been threatened by any circumstance? Did you pray?

Writing references and praises for his help will enhance your intimacy with God.

Other Praises

In Luke 2:14, the angels praised God at Jesus's birth. Simeon praised God for the privilege of seeing and blessing the newborn Messiah (Luke 2:29–32). Anna, an eighty-four-year-old widow who spent her life in fasting and prayer in the temple, praised God for the blessing of seeing the newborn Savior (Luke 2:36–38).

The disciples praised God when Peter was released from prison by the angel (Acts 12).

How have you praised God for delivering you from some prison, either emotional or physical?

How have you praised God for making himself known to you?

Prayer: communicating with God. Is there any higher form of communication available to a human being? Did you notice that the prayer of confession (Daniel 9) and the prayer of love (John 17) are both much longer than the prayer of requests (Matthew 6)?

Remember God will not hear, much less answer, your prayer if you *cherish* sin in your heart (Psalm 66:16–20).

How Does God Talk to Us?

We have looked at communication from the perspective of your prayers to God. Now let's look at communication from God's perspective. The Bible is full of answered prayer. Answered prayer is God communicating with you. The most immediate answer that comes to mind is the one for which California farmers have been praying for the past several years. We have been praying for rain. In central California, where I live, we have already received more rain in this season (winter-spring of 2015–2016) than in all of last year.

God is speaking to you through the rain, communicating his faithfulness and his care for you. In 1 Chronicles 28:9, David charged his son Solomon with the following words: "If you seek him, he will be found by you, but if you forsake him, he will cast you off forever." He is saying that God will respond to your seeking. See also Matthew 7:11.

As mentioned earlier in this chapter, Moses and David prayed frequently, and God spoke to them directly. Isaiah 55:6 says, "Seek the Lord while he may be found: call upon him while he is near." The Lord spoke to the Israelites through Jeremiah 29:12. "Then you will call upon me and come and pray to me, and I will hear you. You will seek me and find me, when you seek me with all your heart. I will be found by you, declares the Lord."

In Daniel 10:2–14, the Lord presents some of the most intimate words about answered prayer. It touches my heart every time I read the passage.

> In those days, I Daniel, was mourning for three weeks. I ate no delicacies, no meat or wine entered my mouth, nor did I anoint myself at all, for the full three weeks … I lifted up my eyes and looked, and behold, a man clothed in linen, with a belt of fine gold from Uphaz around his waist … And he said to me, "O Daniel, man greatly loved, understand the words that I speak to you … Fear not, Daniel, for from the first day that you set your heart to understand and humbled yourself before your God, your words have been heard, and I have come because of your words."

That interaction between a heavenly messenger and Daniel was very special, even for Daniel. The intimacy of the communication between a messenger of God and a human being helps you understand the potential for intimacy with God in your life. The more you seek to humble yourself and "set your heart to understand," the more God will honor your life and your requests. In the Old Testament, the Lord spoke most often through the prophets or the kings. Sometimes he spoke through heavenly messengers. In the New Testament, Christ spoke to many people directly. He often taught in the temple. He fed groups of four thousand and, later, five thousand men, after he had been talking to them of the new way of life. He continues to speak to you through the Holy Spirit, through his Word, and through nature. He is always communicating.

Are you always listening?

The Goal

The goal of this chapter has been to call to your attention the importance of communicating with God. For everyone, including Jesus, prayer is essential.

Prayer is an act of obedience, worship, need, and thanksgiving, all at the same time. If you think it might be a difficult form of communication to develop, look again at the Lord's Prayer. There are four or five simple concepts. Even a child can remember them. Remember Christianity isn't always easy, but it is always simple.

The Lord loves to hear from his children, as do most parents. People rejoice in the development of communication, from baby talk to the language of the Declaration of Independence.

Prayer is the most intimate form of communication with God. How do you celebrate the ability to think about and speak with the living God?

You love to hear that you are loved and to express your love for another. God is your Father and Jesus is your brother, lover, or friend. They want to hear from you. Do you tell them how much you love them?

Pray Without Ceasing

Part 3

WHAT SOMETIMES HAPPENS

All we like sheep have gone astray;
we have turned—every one—to his own way.
—Isaiah 53:6

7

ANXIETY, OR PEACE WITH HIM

Can I be free from anxiety?
I wanted to know.

> The Lord is at hand; do not be anxious about anything, but in everything by prayer and supplication with thanksgiving let your requests be made known to God. And the peace of God, which surpasses all understanding, will guard your hearts and your minds in Christ Jesus.
>
> —Philippians 4:6–7

"Do not be anxious about anything." Surely, he must be kidding. In the previous chapter, we learned how significant prayer is. Here, God says to pray about everything. Some of you may not be troubled by anxiety. For one who had experienced anxiety since the age of ten, being free of it seemed impossible except for the will and power of God. Perhaps you have been well protected and have never experienced anxiety; you have always felt secure. If that is you, you have been truly blessed. This is a good time to praise him.

In *It's All about Him*, I gave *Merriam-Webster's* definition of anxiety: stress about something *that does not exist in the moment*[33] (Brittell 2014,

---

[33] *Merriam-Webster's Collegiate Dictionary*, 11th ed., s.v. "anxiety."

92). Did you read that? Anxiety is about something that does not exist in the moment. It may have happened in the past, or it may happen in the future, but it is not happening now.

If it doesn't exist, why am I so stressed about it?

Anxiety is one of the most frequent diagnoses in our culture right now. People at all levels of society are feeling anxious, worried about something that does not exist. Many people are on medication. More than many disorders, anxiety is sin because God says not to be anxious. What is psychologically fascinating is that all this tension is about something that does not exist. Since God knows both the future and the past, he says, "Don't go there."

It's All about Him gives a more detailed account of symptoms that may accompany anxiety, including restlessness, fatigue, difficulty concentrating, irritability, muscle tension, and sleep disturbance (Brittell 2014, 92).

If you struggle with anxiety, do you have any of these feelings? If so, which ones?

How often?

How long do these symptoms last: hours, days, weeks, months, years, or decades?

What Causes Anxiety?

A major cause of anxiety is the loss of security or fearing the loss of security. The anxiety can result from feelings of abandonment, abuse, lack of love, rejection, overt hatred, or severe trauma. Any of these experiences can precipitate intense anxiety. *It's All about Him* describes the physical loss of support in infants as the "startle response" (Brittell 2014, 93). In adult years, loss of emotional support often expresses itself in the soul (psyche, emotions) as feelings of anxiety or depression and may also feel emotionally startling. Given the chaos in relationships caused by adultery, divorce, abuse, rape, drug abuse, and other tearing disruptions, it is no wonder there is a high level of anxiety and depression in the culture. Other causes include learned behavior or sin, either personal sin or someone else's sin against you. Certain medications or physical disorders can also cause anxiety.

Anxiety relies largely on emotional memory. Remembering something from the past or anticipating something in the future can trigger strong emotional responses. I can bring some circumstance into my awareness and then start ruminating about it. "What if … If only … I wish I had …" The passage most likely to prevent this is found in the modeling of Paul, where he says we are to take every thought captive (2 Corinthians 10:5).

How good are you at taking your thoughts captive? Do you think it is something only others can do? Remember the command to be transformed by the renewing of your mind is a universal command for the born-again (Romans 12:2).

Read Matthew 6:25–34, Luke 12:22–32, and Philippians 4:6–7. They are, perhaps, the most comprehensive passages addressing the cure for anxiety.

If you have experienced anxiety, which of the things listed do you see as being objects of your anxiety? Where do you fall on the spectrum? How often do you worry about any of these?

- food
- drink
- clothing

Are you worrying about the length of your life or about dying? The Lord has picked the day of your death (Psalm 139:16). If it is your day, whether you are crossing the ocean in an airplane or peeling bananas in your kitchen, you will be called home. How do you feel about that?

Since God is taking care of all your needs and has picked the day of your death, what can your worrying or anxiety add to his care (Philippians 4:19)?

The Difference between Anxiety and Fear

Fear can elicit many of the same feelings as anxiety, but there is an objective reason for the fear, usually the presence of danger. The distinction between anxiety and fear is the difference between something that is not real in the present moment—something imaginary, a future anticipation, or a memory—and something dangerous that is both very real and an imminent threat. A shadow is a good example of something that can cause anxiety. A shadow cannot cause any real harm. The person or object creating the shadow may be able to cause you great harm, but the shadow itself cannot accomplish anything real. It is only representative of something that is real.

A shadow is similar to a memory: the event that caused the memory may have been very real and painful, but the memory itself is not dangerous unless you allow it to take control of your thought processes. It is only an activity of your mind over which you can take control. There is nothing in the cause for anxiety—whether memory, shadow, or anticipation—that is creating any real harm in the moment. However, the anticipation, shadow, or memory can cause a great deal of distress. In the case of anxiety, it is *essential* to take one's thoughts captive to Christ.

Fear, on the other hand, is a reaction to a real or present danger. It is caused by something real. If someone is holding a knife to your throat, fear is normal. You may be afraid of being murdered or tortured. Fear may motivate you to action. You might cry out, thereby attracting attention and bringing help, or you might run and seek to escape.

Fear is about something that is happening in the present. In addition to the passages commanding you not to fear, many refer to the Lord as your rock, your shield, your fortress, and a safe place (Psalm 18:1–2). You live in a time of significant distress in the world. As always, you need to stay close to him and be obedient to his commands, including the command not to allow fear or anxiety to take control of your emotions or thought processes.

God says, "Fear not." Why not? With so much chaos in the world, why not be afraid? In Genesis 15:1, God said to Abram, "Fear not … I am your shield." To Hagar, the angel said, "Fear not, for God has heard" (Genesis 21:17). God said to Isaac, "Fear not, for I am with you and will bless you" (Genesis 26:24). In Exodus 14:13, Moses said to the Israelites, "Fear not, stand firm, and see the salvation of the Lord." "But the Lord said to Moses, 'Do not fear him'" (Numbers 21:34). Deuteronomy 1:21 says, "Do not fear or be dismayed." Again in Deuteronomy 31:6–8, Moses said to Joshua and the people,

> Be strong and courageous, do not fear or be in dread of them, for it is the Lord your God who goes with you. He will not leave you or forsake you … It is the Lord who goes before you; he will be with you. He will not leave you or forsake you. Do not fear or be dismayed.

This is my favorite:

> Fear not for I am with you; be not dismayed, for I am your God; I will strengthen you, I will help you, I will uphold you with my righteous *right hand* … For I, the Lord your God hold your *right hand*; it is I who say to you, "Fear not, I am the one who helps you."
> —Isaiah 41:10 and 13 (emphasis added)

The right hands are clasped. His right hand is holding your right hand. What can be safer than that? What is your reaction to these passages?

In Psalm 18:2, David says to the Lord that He is

- my rock

- my fortress

- my deliverer

- my God

- my shield

- the horn of my salvation

- my stronghold

These are just a few of the words where the Lord assures you that he is your security. It will be well worth your time to get a large concordance and study all of them. These verses would be beneficial to internalize so that when the enemy tries to tempt you to fear or be anxious you have the truth inside you.

What the Bible Says about a Cure

When God says, "Do not be anxious" or "Do not fear," he must have a way not to be anxious or fearful. He doesn't say not to have allergies or asthma. He must have a plan to counteract anxiety and fear. In Mark 5:35, Jesus says to Jairus, "Do not fear, only believe." To us, his disciples, he says, "Fear not little flock, for it is your Father's good pleasure to give you the kingdom" (Luke 12:32). First John 4:16–19 says, "There is no fear in love, but perfect love casts out fear ... We love because he first loved us." These passages give us instruction, in addition to the passage in Philippians 4 that says to pray. So you get four prescriptions: *believe, be obedient, love,* and *pray.* These will lead to peace.

What feelings are you having?

I had five years of psychotherapy with three different therapists using three different methods of treatment. I was still troubled by anxiety. Then I started doing what God says to do in Philippians 4:6. "Pray about everything." It is interesting how obedience is always rewarded.

Starting with one to three minutes a day—as long as I could stay focused—and increasing to waiting on God for eight hours a day, changed my life. You *can* learn to control your thoughts. You *can* learn to recognize his voice. You *can* learn to pray about everything.

I prayed about what to eat, what to wear, what to do, and what to say to my patients. Everything I did in a day became an object of prayer. Though I am now retired, I try to maintain the habit of praying about everything, asking God how he wants me to spend the day he has given me. He really does listen for as long as you are seeking him. You may leave him, but he will never "leave you or forsake you" (Deuteronomy 31:6).

Read the first part of that Philippians 4 passage, starting with verse 4. Rejoice, be reasonable, and *realize the Lord is at hand.* If you followed those three commands, most of your anxiety would be relieved. Then, pray about everything. What a combination of cures! As mentioned in verse 7, "The peace of God which passes all understanding will guard your hearts and minds in Christ Jesus." It really happens! It may not make sense, it may be beyond your understanding, but he can cause it to happen.

List some times when God caused circumstances to change in such a way that peace was beyond your understanding. Make a list of things God has done for you or given you that are beyond your understanding.

My Story

As mentioned earlier, I had been anxious since I was ten. At that time, a traumatic event occurred that left me feeling constantly anxious. I was never sure I was doing the right thing or that I was in the will of God. I was a deeply spiritual and sensitive child from early in life. Many things became issues for me that seemed insignificant for other children. Two years earlier, I had been born again when my father prayed with me to accept what Christ had done for me. Following the traumatic event, I began to wonder whether I was really a Christian. I had nightmares, my posture changed, and I was never sure of anything. By God's grace, I was a good student and enjoyed school and learning. Studying and learning became an escape, a comfort, and reassuring.

By the time I was in high school, I realized that it was my privilege and my obligation to do as well as possible in my studies. My mother insisted that my homework always came first, ahead of chores and playtime. The development of this habit served me well throughout my life, even in later years.

I married a widower with two daughters. When the girls were grown, the opportunity to go back to school became a reality. I was able to go back to school, ultimately obtaining my doctorate in psychology. During all these years, I was never sure of anything: whether to marry or not, whether the work I was doing was what God wanted me to do, or whether I was good enough for anything or anyone.

My graduate program required me to have a certain number of hours of individual psychotherapy. During my second therapy, I asked my therapist why I was always in so much pain. (It was Freudian therapy; usually there was no input from the therapist.) This was the one time he spoke to me in two and a half years of twice weekly therapy. He said, "Massive insecurity." Finally, the pain and anxiety had a name: massive insecurity.

Security

Security means "freedom from danger, fear, or anxiety."[34] In *It's All about Him,* I list several passages that deal with security (Brittell 2014, 100–101). I will quote a few of them here. Be sure to internalize some of them.

> Be strong and courageous. Do not fear or be in dread of them [anxiety], for it is the Lord your God who goes with you. He will not leave you or forsake you … It is the Lord who goes before you. He will be with you; he will not leave you or forsake you. Do not fear or be dismayed.
> —Deuteronomy 31:6–8

"The beloved of the Lord dwells in safety. The High God surrounds him all day long, and dwells between his shoulders" (Deuteronomy 33:12).

"The Lord your God is in your midst, a mighty one who will save … He will quiet you by his love; he will exult over you with loud singing" (Zephaniah 3:17).

"We who have fled for refuge might have strong encouragement to hold fast to the hope set before us" (Hebrews 6:18).

"So we can confidently say, 'The Lord is my helper; I will not fear, what can man do to me?'" (Hebrews 13:6).

What did you learn from studying these passages and the context in which they were written?

---

[34] *Merriam-Webster's Collegiate Dictionary*, 11th ed., s.v. "security."

After studying them, record some of the changes that have taken place in your thinking and feeling. Write your story as you have experienced it up to this point in your life. Record changes in thought and emotions that you feel capable of making after studying this chapter and the biblical references both in this book and in *It's All about Him* (Brittell 2014, 100–101).

The Goal

The goal of this chapter was to help you choose freedom from anxiety and fear. The Lord has provided so many ways to *not be anxious or fearful*. It is possible to live an anxiety-free life as long as you are obedient to his cure. He will give you the peace "which surpasses all understanding." It will guard your heart and mind in Christ Jesus. He says to believe, obey, love, and pray. Then you will have peace.

Only in knowing and submitting to Christ will you find total security. It may take time to change habits of anxiety and fear. However, he will always be with you and never forsake you. Persevere in turning your anxieties and fears into something that is reasonable, rejoice, and then pray about it. It may be a lifetime process. Begin today.

People are often critical of the process of labeling. However, giving something a name can be very helpful. We give and are given names. They become part of our identity. In the same way, having a name for what is tormenting a person can help one think more accurately about what is going on internally and how to overcome it. Pray about everything.

Have No Anxiety: Fear Not.

8

Depression, or Contentment with Him

**How can I be content?
I wanted to know.**

> Not that I am speaking of being in need, for I have learned in whatever situation I am to be content. I know how to be brought low, and I know how to abound. In any and every circumstance, I have learned the secret of facing plenty and hunger, abundance and need. I can do all things through him who strengthens me [Paul].
>
> —Philippians 4:11–13

Contentment

To be *content* is "to limit (oneself) in requirements, desires, or actions."[35] Vine defines contentment as "to be possessed of sufficient strength, to be strong, to be enough for a thing."[36] Paul said he had learned to have sufficient strength to endure what he was experiencing.

---

[35] *Merriam-Webster's Collegiate Dictionary*, 11th ed., s.v. "content."

[36] *Vine's Concise Dictionary*, s.v. "content."

"And my God will supply every need of yours according to his riches in glory in Christ Jesus," wrote Paul while he was in prison awaiting execution (Philippians 4:19). He had persecuted and participated in the killing of many Christians, so when it says you reap what you sow, Paul had a great deal of reaping to do (Galatians 6:7). Perhaps that was part of his contentment. You reap the joy of your faithfulness as well as the consequences of your sin. It is worth your time to read 2 Corinthians 11:24–28 to refresh your memory regarding all the persecutions Paul endured. Through all the torments, he remained content with God. He did not become depressed. God always gives grace for the reaping.

Depression

The symptoms of depression are adequately described in *It's All about Him* (Brittell 2014, 103–104). They include poor concentration, low energy, low self-esteem, and feelings of hopelessness. A depressed person often expresses a wish to die. *Depression* is defined as a feeling of dejection or hopelessness.[37] What is important is to explore whether what is being felt and expressed is truly depression—often based in anger—or godly sorrow that can lead to repentance. Or is it sadness from loss, often called grieving or mourning. The pain of loss, if not dealt with appropriately, can turn into anger and depression. If you have been dependent on or had a close relationship with a person whom you have lost, grief can be intense.

Perhaps the greatest difficulty in working with depression comes when anger is confused with sorrow, sadness, or grief. Attempting to treat depression without exploring sorrow, sadness, and grief can make the problem worse. It is essential that both anger and loss be explored to determine the ultimate cause of the distress.

Anger is often a second-level emotion based on pain. Pain is most uncomfortable. You may try to medicate the pain away. Anger is more comfortable since there are many outlets for expressing anger. In the early days of psychology, depression was defined as anger turned inward or

---

[37] *Merriam-Webster's Collegiate Dictionary*, 11th ed., s.v. "depression."

frozen rage. One of my hopes in writing this chapter is to help people grieve their losses so that grief does not turn into anger and become depression. Loss of hope or of a dream or plan can be as devastating as the loss of a person. In a later chapter, we will look at hope. God commands us to have hope in him. If we try to have hope in someone or something apart from God, there is sure to be disappointment that can lead to depression.

Some Who Were Sad

It's All about Him presents several examples of people who grieved intensely after the loss of a loved one (Brittell 2014, 108–109). Abraham mourned and wept at the death of Sarah (Genesis 23:2). At the death of Moses, the Israelites wept for thirty days (Deuteronomy 34:8). At the death of Jonathan and Saul, David and the men with him tore their clothes, wept, and fasted. David wrote a very touching lament for Jonathan (2 Samuel 1:17–27). Scripture deals with loss in death, including Jesus's death, as a painful and significant event and presents mourning as an appropriate response. In ancient times, the bereaved sometimes called for professional mourners to help express the pain.

Job experienced loss at a level rarely experienced in human history. Read his story in the book of Job. It is best to read the entire book to understand what was really going on. He lost his family, his wealth, his health, and his earthly security, all at Satan's request. In verses 20–22 of Job 1, you have the description of his reaction. "Then Job arose and tore his robe and shaved his head and fell on the ground and *worshipped*" (emphasis added). This is not the reaction of an angry man but of a man who is overwhelmed by grief. His wife, on the other hand, was angry. She suggested that he "curse God and die" (Job 2:9). Job, however, maintained his integrity and did not sin (Job 2:10). Anguish! Could anything be more devastating? Yet you do not hear anger, just pain. You do not hear self-pity. You do not hear blaming God. You hear great sorrow.

What would you have done?

Have you lost a loved one or suffered some other great loss? If so, have you taken the time to grieve? Did you cry and, perhaps, wail?

If not, how did you express your grief? Did it bring relief?

Were you left with regrets at their passing or leaving?

How did you deal with those?

It is very important to look for and deal with any grief that may have been unexplored in a depressed person's life. The Lord speaks of the lost sheep, the lost coin, and lost people. Loss almost always triggers a response that may include grief. Be careful not to confuse anger with grief.

Depression can be medicated for years. Unless the original pain of loss is dealt with, very little will change except the nature of the mood. Medication is designed to alter mood, which it can do.

In the section on page 109 of *It's All about Him,* I have listed some of our cultural expectations (Brittell 2014). Look through them to determine which apply to you. Unfulfilled expectations can be a source of large amounts of grief that often turn to anger.

What expectations do you recognize in your own life?

Which of them have not been fulfilled?

How have you grieved those losses?

Are you angry that they were not fulfilled? How have you dealt with the anger?

In my clinical practice, I frequently encountered this fantasy: "I married my opposite, but my spouse should change to be like me." Patients frequently expected their partners to know their unexpressed wants and needs. Only God can do that.

Look into your own heart. See if there is an unwarranted expectation (fantasy) lurking there, causing dissatisfaction and, ultimately, depression. With your focus on the Lord and perhaps some professional help, you may be able to give up the fantasy that is keeping you bound and unhappy. Give it a try. Remember Paul was able to be content in prison after having been tortured. He kept his focus on God. Few of us will go through what Paul endured. But then, few of us will torture as many Christians as Paul did. The Lord always gives mercy to endure the reaping.

Start by writing down as many unrealistic expectations (fantasies) as you can think of.

If you need professional help to work through these fantasies, get it. However, if you are a Christian, make sure that any professional with whom you work has a Christian belief system. Some secular therapists believe that developing fantasies is healthy. This is not in agreement with the gospel. The gospel is based on the fact that Jesus is the truth and the Holy Spirit is the Spirit of truth.

When you find key words in your fantasies, look them up in your concordance. See what God says about them.

How have you remained content with God when you have gone through very difficult times?

Did you recognize the relationship between what you were going through and some past sins for which these times might be the reaping? If so, write them down and look them up in your concordance to see what God says about them.

Some Who Were Angry

The Old Testament gives us insights into the lives of several of the prophets who might be considered to have been depressed. Jonah is the clearest example of buried anger. He was angry. If he obeyed God, the people of Nineveh might repent and be saved. What a cause for anger in a prophet! He went so far as to ask the sailors of the ship in which he was trying to escape God's call on his life to throw him overboard. They did. God rescued him by sending a big fish to swallow Jonah. As the story moves toward its climax, Jonah's anger becomes obvious. When God asks him if he has a right to be angry, he declares that he does; he "is angry enough to die" (Jonah 4:9). No part of the story shows Jonah dealing with his anger in any appropriate way (Jonah 1–4).

Elijah, another of God's prophets, clearly told God why he was angry (1 Kings 19). Hungry, exhausted, and feeling alone, abandoned, and a bit self-righteous, he asked the Lord if he could die. Instead, the Lord set him free by feeding him, giving him rest, and explaining the truth about the situation. As the Lord says, the truth shall set you free (John 8:32). Remember Job. He trusted God without understanding the circumstances.

Jeremiah, a prophet, was angry. He felt the Lord had deceived him. He actually asked God whether God was going to deceive him (Jeremiah 15:18). He beautifully described how he felt when he didn't preach God's

Word that he had been commanded to deliver (Jeremiah 20:9). When the Lord brought vengeance on his persecutors, Jeremiah was no longer depressed. Justice fulfilled can be a great source of encouragement as well as relieving anger and depression.

Have you ever been angry? Describe how you felt.

Have you ever been angry with God? Did you tell him how angry you were and how you felt?

Have you ever attempted to take your life or asked God to take it? If you made a suicide attempt, are you grateful that it wasn't successful?

Toward a Biblical Cure

Scripture teaches how to deal with anger correctly. Ephesians 4:25–32 gives several instructions on how to live so that you can have victory over anger and depression. You are to take the anger off; remove it as you would a coat. You have control over whether you are going to indulge it or remove it from your life. The following instructions are quoted in *It's All about Him* (Brittell 2014, 111) but bear repeating:

- Speak the truth.
- Don't let the sun go down on your anger.
- Don't give the Devil a foothold.
- Don't let any unwholesome word come out of your mouth.
- Do not grieve the Holy Spirit of God.
- Get rid of all bitterness, rage, anger, brawling, slander, and malice.

In Joel 2:12–13, the Lord says,

> Return to me with all your heart, with fasting, with weeping, and with mourning; and rend your hearts and not your garments. Return to the Lord your God, for he is gracious and merciful, slow to anger, and abounding in steadfast love.

That is the clearest path to wholeness.

Forgive and seek forgiveness. Don't let your anger turn into bitterness and depression. If you are stuck in a wound from childhood, forgive the perpetrator and let your mind be transformed by thinking about it in light of what Christ has done for you. If you need professional help to overcome the pain, seek a Christian pastor or counselor to give you guidance.

One passage of scripture can have a strong impact on depression if you practice it consistently.

> Finally brothers whatever is true, whatever is honorable, whatever is just, whatever is pure, whatever is lovely, whatever is commendable, if there is any excellence, if there is anything worthy of praise, think about these things.
> —Philippians 4:8

In an earlier chapter, I emphasized that you can learn to control your thoughts. In fact, you are commanded to take your thoughts captive to Christ (Ephesians 10:5). Roman 12:2 says that you are to be transformed by renewing your mind. You can and must learn to think differently about your experiences if you want to live the abundant life for which Christ came (John 10:10).

> "Therefore lift your drooping hands and strengthen your weak knees, and make straight paths for your feet, so that what is lame may not be put out of joint, but rather be healed" (Hebrews 12:12–13).

Changing your thought patterns can relieve a lot of the anger and depression.

Recently I was discussing an event in my life with my mentor. He pointed out that what I interpreted as punishment had, in fact, been a warning. Had I heeded the warning, I would have been spared a great deal of pain.

Cognitive behavioral therapy (CBT) suggests that it is not what happened to you but how you interpret what happened that results in pain, anxiety, and depression. As a Christian, you are to interpret things through the template of Christ's death and resurrection and the impact that has had on the whole of history and on your life. You have been given the Holy Spirit as a helper and comforter. You have eternal life with God. Reinterpreting whatever sin has been done against you in the light of what Christ has done for you will help you let go of your anger, whether it is over a physical, psychological, or spiritual injury. Jesus gave his life so you might be healed of your injury (Isaiah 53:5).

Lack of forgiveness is a major contributing factor in the development of depression. Everyone has been sinned against at one time or another. Holding on to the memory of a painful event and allowing bitterness to develop is a sure way to become depressed. "See to it that no one fails to obtain the grace of God; that no root of bitterness springs up and causes trouble, and by it many become defiled" (Hebrews 12:15).

Look into your heart again. What are you holding on to that you could, by the grace of God, forgive?

Against whom have you sinned? What can you do to seek their forgiveness?

Do whatever needs to be done to let it go, whether that includes confrontation, lots of prayer, repentance, or forgiving someone. God has called you to be content and has made provision for you to be able to live in contentment.

A percentage of depression is organic in nature and those cases need medical treatment. As mentioned in *It's All about Him*, your thought patterns can alter the course of that disorder as well (Brittell 2014, 105.)

The Goal

The goal of this chapter is to help you recognize the difference between depression that is resulting from anger, or sadness from sin, grief, or loss. This distinction is very significant.

Depression can result from poor physical conditions as well as poverty or physical illness. Anger may result from a lack of either understanding or knowledge relevant to the situation.

In *It's All about Him*, I shared the story of a young male patient (Brittell 2014, 113). Having been told something was chemically wrong with his brain, he was put on medication because he was very sad, almost despondent. When he was able to share his grief and have it validated in treatment, he made a wonderful recovery.

Forgiveness, repentance, grieving, and putting off anger are God ordained. Depression is not. God has made appropriate provision for dealing with our sin, pain, grief, and anger. He says, "Be still and know that I am God" (Psalm 46:10). You can live in contentment. Paul modeled it.

Think On Things That Are Excellent

9

ARROGANCE, OR HUMILITY BEFORE HIM

**How can I humble myself?
I wanted to know.**

> Have this mind among yourselves, which is yours in Christ
> Jesus, who though he was in the form of God did not count
> equality with God a thing to be grasped but made himself
> nothing, taking the form of a servant ... And being found in
> human form, he humbled himself by becoming obedient to the
> point of death, even death on a cross.
>
> —Philippians 2:5–8

It is not possible to humble oneself to any greater degree than Christ
did. He left his home in heaven to come to earth to be born, live, and die
as a human being, then to be supernaturally resurrected for you. Consider
his humility, awareness, and awesomeness. His humility was based on his
obedience. Read the whole passage in Philippians 2:5–11.

Have this mind-set within you. *Humility* is defined as not being proud,
haughty, or arrogant but having a spirit of submission.[38] Vine defines the

---

[38] *Merriam-Webster's Collegiate Dictionary*, 11th ed., s.v. "humility."

word *humble* as "to become low, to be abased."[39] Humility is neither a fruit of the Spirit nor a gift of the Spirit. Nor is it an emotion. It is a choice of the will, to be practiced. "Humble yourselves, therefore, under the mighty hand of God" (1 Peter 5:6). It is an imperative, the result of choosing obedience. Jesus chose to obey. You have the choice to obey or disobey. You will, however, live with the consequences of your choice, even as he did in returning to his home in heaven.

How comfortable do you feel humbling yourself?

I recall one Sunday when a good friend approached me after church. She told me she had dreamed about me. In the dream, I had been wearing a brooch in the shape of a brain on my shoulder. Well, I had just been awarded my PhD in psychology. I was feeling grateful and proud that I had been able to accomplish all that was required to reach that goal. The Lord spoke to me and said, "How did you manage to accomplish all this?"

"Well, you gave me a good brain," I answered. Then I remembered I cannot even breathe without his permission (Job 12:10). By his grace, I chose to humble myself.

Is humbling yourself easy? Perhaps not. Is it commanded? Yes.

Everyone struggles with this. Christianity isn't always easy, but it is always simple. Choose to obey. You might want to make notes of this one to help you remember how you did it this time. In all likelihood, it will need to be a recurring choice.

---

[39] *Vine's Concise Dictionary*, s.v. "humble."

What Should Be the Basis for Our Humility?

Paul, in 1 Corinthians 4:7, says it best. "What do you have that you did not receive? If then you received it, why do you boast as if you did not receive it?" Can it be any simpler than this? Life and his blessings are all gifts from the living God. Humility is a lifelong choice that you must practice constantly in light of God's grace.

What is your response?

With which of God's gifts are you especially pleased?

How do you express humility in those circumstances?

What are some of the gifts he has given you with which you are not so pleased?

How do you respond in humility in those circumstances?

What Does Humility Look Like?

At the age of twelve, Jesus humbled himself and remained in submission to his parents. After his parents found their twelve-year-old son in the temple interacting with teachers and doctors of the law, he went home with his parents, obeyed them, and lived under their control until he was approximately thirty years old. That is submission, a large part of humility!

He submitted to being tempted by the Devil (Luke 4). How humiliating to have to interact with Satan, whom he could have annihilated by his breath. Jesus humbled himself with his mother and siblings. They thought he was out of his mind (Mark 3:21). He didn't use his power to correct them, which he could easily have done. He just corrected their opinion on the importance of relationships. He submitted to his disciples by washing their feet (John 13). He submitted to his Father by coming to earth and living and dying for us. That is a lot of submission. That is a lot of humility.

What Does Arrogance Look Like?

Arrogance means an attitude of superiority, an overbearing manner.[40] Arrogance appears to have begun in heaven when Satan exalted himself, wanting to be as the Most High. He was a created angel. He could not have changed to another form of being. He did manage to change the course of human history through one simple conversation with Eve. Eve succumbed to his charm. If angels can be so misguided by pride and arrogance, how much more can you and I be vulnerable and misguided? Proverbs 4:23 says to guard your heart. Jesus says out of the heart come all kinds of evil (Matthew 12:34). David says, "I will not set before my eyes anything that is worthless" (Psalm 101:3).

In the early twentieth century, philosophers declared that God was dead. How incredibly arrogant and stupid! For a human made of dust to declare his Creator dead, and therefore impotent, seems to be the height of arrogance. Again, God could have annihilated them with the breath of his mouth. Philosophers replaced God in their imaginations with various emphases, one of which was the *self.* I invite you to look in the dictionary for all the *self*-words that have been developed. It is astonishing to see all of them in a group.

Another emphasis that emerged during this time was the emphasis on emotions. If you felt it, you had the *right* to express it and to act on it. The degree to which we humans have become arrogant is tragic. In today's culture, there are protests of all kinds and descriptions. The Bible says to honor your government officials. Protestors have sunk to a new low by encouraging people to kill police. A whole culture or nation can lose its

---

[40] *Merriam-Webster's Collegiate Dictionary*, 11th ed., s.v. "arrogance."

way without God. Newscasters say that the majority of people in our own country feel that our country is on the wrong track. We have removed God from our schools and from as many other places as possible. Without God, we cannot help but lose the truth. Life without truth can be truly terrifying.

Find Scripture passages that support the concept that without God a whole nation can be lost.

Pride and arrogance are judged and condemned throughout Scripture. Think of Satan cast out of heaven; Adam and Eve cast out of the garden; Nebuchadnezzar removed from his throne to eat grass like an ox (Daniel 4); or Peter, who had said he would never deny the Lord, denying three times that he knew him. (Peter was judged but not condemned. He was restored to full relationship with the Lord. Nebuchadnezzar experienced consequences but was restored to his throne when he came to his senses and worshipped God.)

The Lord does, eventually, get tired of man's arrogance. Genesis 6:5–6 says,

> The Lord saw that the wickedness of man was great in the earth, and that every intention of the thoughts of his heart was only evil continually. And the Lord was sorry that he had made man on the earth, and it grieved him to his heart.

Imagine God grieving because of the evil of man. How arrogant of us! He sent the flood, which destroyed all living things.

What are your thoughts on the flood and its impact on the earth?

Write down some examples of those who, in your own lifetime, were humbled when their arrogance became too great to be tolerated by God.

Make a list of prominent people who are currently exalting themselves.

Among your circle of friends, who is attempting to exalt himself or herself?

How are you attempting to exalt yourself?

Why is humility so hard? What are your thoughts?

I've tried to answer that question for myself. Why do I find it so difficult to realistically assess who God made me to be and not try to go above and beyond that? If God thought this was good, why am I not satisfied with his handiwork? I realize it is because I don't trust him. Do you trust him?

If, as you are answering for yourself, you would like to share your thoughts with me, I would be happy to hear from you. I will be establishing a web site.

Arrogance can be a powerful motivator in your life. As noted earlier it is defined as "an attitude of superiority manifested in an overbearing manner or *presumptuous claims*."[41] It is Satan's original sin. "I will make myself as the Most High" (Isaiah 14:14). There is a problem in that statement. He could not remake himself as the Most High. God created Satan to be

---

[41] *Merriam-Webster's Collegiate Dictionary*, 11th ed., s.v. "arrogance."

what he is. Nor can we recreate ourselves to be something higher, bigger, or better than God made us. Eve was hoping to be able to do that after her conversation with Satan (Genesis 3). That didn't work out very well!

How have you tried to be something other than you are, either positively or negatively?

How did that work out?

Are you dissatisfied with how God made you?

Take some time to do some real soul-searching. Dissatisfaction with what God has done is trouble enough. But when you try to be God and try to recreate yourself, you get into real hazard. The contrast to this is to praise God that you are "fearfully and wonderfully made" (Psalm 139). In my clinical work, I encountered so many people who were dissatisfied with some aspect of their being. I am not talking here about the ravages of sin in the world and its impact on a person's body, soul, mind, and heart, although that came into play as well. I am talking about dissatisfaction with the God-given aspects of one's being. Arrogance can be a big part of ingratitude.

What is your greatest vulnerability?

What causes you the most dissatisfaction? Be a bit ruthless with yourself. The point of self-examination is to learn to praise God in all things.

As I am writing this, the city of Paris, France, is attempting to recover from one of the worst terrorist attacks in modern history. The United States is recovering from the worst terrorist attack on the homeland since 9/11. Terrorism, and the barbarism that accompanies it, are two of the most flagrant examples of arrogance in modern times. The terrorist thinks he or she can execute anyone for any cause at any time. Without knowledge of the true God, arrogance knows no bounds. Arrogance is one of the clearest examples of the work of Satan. He started it.

The Lord Promises Reward for Humility: Exaltation

To *exalt* means to "raise in rank, power or character, to elevate by praise."[42] The Lord promises to exalt you if you will humble yourself, "so that at the proper time he may exalt you" (1 Peter 5:6).

What does it look like to be exalted by God? *It's All about Him* lists several people who were exalted for their humility (Brittell 2014, 122–124). Among them are Noah, whom he spared from the flood; Abraham, whom God made the father of many nations and through whom he has promised to bless all nations; Joseph, whom he made the ruler of Egypt; and Moses, to whom God spoke face-to-face as a man speaks to his friend. David was called a man after God's own heart. Daniel was so humble, and such a profound witness to the king of Babylon, that the king acknowledged the Lord God as the true God and said in Daniel 4:3,

How great are his signs,
How mighty his wonders!
His kingdom is an everlasting kingdom
And his dominion endures from generation to generation.

Isaiah was asked to walk around naked and to prophesy for three years (Isaiah 20). Hosea was asked to marry a prostitute and to have her bear his children. When she left him, he had to take her back (Hosea 1). I think these demands took special humility and grace. God exalted these for their obedience.

---

42   *Merriam-Webster's Collegiate Dictionary*, 11th ed., s.v. "exalt."

In the New Testament, Mary withstood criticism for being an unwed mother. One centurion had more faith than anyone Jesus had met in Israel (Matthew 8). We see the man whose friends let him down through the roof and whose sins were forgiven (Matthew 9) and the woman whose faith made her well (Matthew 9). All these people humbled themselves and were exalted by God.

Following a wonderful healing at Lystra, the citizens wanted to worship and offer a sacrifice to Paul and Barnabas (Acts 14). Paul and Barnabas humbled themselves and withstood the people's desires to offer worship and sacrifices to them. They reassured the people that they, themselves, were human and so restrained them. Paul and Barnabas humbled themselves and were exalted by God.

How would you want God to exalt you? Again, be as honest as possible. What you write is not for publication but for the sake of growing in humility.

Can you think of world leaders who exalted themselves and how that self-exaltation impacted the world? Write down how that has impacted your world.

Can you think of any who are currently exalting themselves? Record how their arrogance impacts your world.

Which of your friends are attempting to exalt themselves?

In what way are you attempting to exalt yourself?

Why is humility so hard?

I have had to answer these questions for myself. Why do I find it so difficult to realistically assess who God made me to be and not try to present myself above and beyond that? *I realize it is because I don't trust his love for me.*

Self-Exaltation

A list of those who tried to exalt themselves in the Bible includes the most famous one: Satan. For his efforts, he was thrown out of heaven and took a third of the angels with him. They, too, must have had a problem with self-exaltation. The following examples clearly show people who tried to exalt themselves by killing someone.

How could becoming a murderer possibly exalt a person? You would achieve notoriety, perhaps, but exaltation?

Cain tried to exalt himself in presenting his offering to the Lord. When God did not honor his offering in the same way he had Abel's, Cain killed his brother (Genesis 4). Moses killed an Egyptian who was abusing an Israelite (Exodus 2). David had the husband of the woman he had taken killed (2 Samuel 11). Haman, in the court of Ahasuerus, went to extraordinary lengths to exalt himself. In the end, he was hanged on the gallows he had prepared for Mordecai, the Jew, who had been instrumental in saving the king's life (Esther 1–10).

Murder is perhaps the most appalling form of self-exaltation. In a study of self-esteem referenced in *It's All about Him*, criminals had very high levels of self-esteem (Brittell 2014, 117).

Joseph's brothers exalted themselves and sold Joseph into slavery (Genesis 37). They had planned to kill him but thought better of it. Aaron and Miriam, Moses's siblings, tried to exalt themselves. Miriam was made leprous for her efforts (Numbers 12). King Saul, the first king of Israel, exalted himself in disobedience. As a result, he lost both his kingdom and the presence of the Holy Spirit in his life (1 Samuel). Many people in the Old Testament tried to exalt themselves.

In the New Testament, Ananias and Sapphira are the classic example of two people who lied to exalt what they had done, attempting to aggrandize themselves (Acts 5). Instead of being exalted, they dropped dead in their tracks, first Ananias and then Sapphira.

Look for others in the Scripture and your concordance. Look at how miserably they failed. What do you get as the lesson from all this arrogance?

As I write this, scores of Parisians, thousands of Americans, many Christians, and many Muslims have been murdered and hundreds injured by attacks. How were the perpetrators trying to exalt themselves?

God's Exaltation

> He leads the humble in what is right, and teaches the humble his way.
> —Psalm 25:9

> When the humble see it, they will be glad; you who seek God, let your hearts revive.
> —Psalm 69:3

> One's pride will bring him low, but he who is lowly in spirit will obtain honor.
> —Proverbs 29:23

> Then he said to me, "Fear not Daniel, for from the first day that you set your heart to understand and humbled yourself before your God, your words have been heard, and I have come because of your words."

—Daniel 10:12

The greatest among you shall be your servant. Whoever exalts himself will be humbled, and whoever humbles himself will be exalted.

—Matthew 23:11–12

He has shown strength with his arm; he has scattered the proud in the thoughts of their hearts; he has brought down the mighty from their thrones and exalted those of humble estate.

—Luke 1:51–52

For by the grace given to me I say to everyone among you not to think of himself more highly than he ought to think, but to think with sober judgment.

—Romans 12:3

God opposes the proud, but gives grace to the humble … Humble yourselves before the Lord and he will exalt you.

—James 4:6, 10

Clothe yourselves, all of you, with humility toward one another, for God opposes the proud, but gives grace to the humble. Humble yourselves, therefore, under the mighty hand of God, so that at the proper time he may exalt you.

—1 Peter 5:5–6

Since everything you have is a gift from God, when would arrogance or pride ever be legitimate? Record some temptations to be arrogant.

The Goal

The goal of this chapter has been to present the pitfall (sin) of being proud or arrogant. Paul makes it simple to understand: everything you have is a gift. I might add that this gift includes the air you breathe and the ability to breathe it (Job 12:10).

God promises great reward for humbling ourselves. You may not recognize the rewards immediately, but he is always faithful to keep his word. Christ had to live thirty-three years, be crucified, dead, buried, and resurrected before he was able to go back to heaven and obtain his reward.

> Therefore God has highly exalted him and bestowed on him the name that is above every name, so that at the name of Jesus every knee should bow, in heaven and on earth and under the earth, and every tongue confess that Jesus Christ is Lord, to the glory of God the Father.
>
> —Philippians 2:9–11

This chapter lists several of God's promises to reward humility. Spend some time looking for others. Also, look at the lives of those who received their reward for humble obedience, including the Lord. Internalize the quality of humility in their lives.

It is such a thrill to recognize that some event in your own life is the result of the Lord repaying you for your obedience in humility. Record it to help you remember its significance.

Humility Is A Choice

Part 4

RESTORATION IN HIM

And we know that for those who love God all things work together for good, for those who are called according to his purpose.
—Romans 8:28

10

DETACHMENT, OR TRUST IN HIM

**Would I ever be able to feel again?
I wanted to know.**

Trust in the Lord with all your heart, and do
not lean on your own understanding.
—Proverbs 3:5

Definitions

To *detach* means to separate from.[43] Psychological detachment means separating one's emotions from what is going on in the real world. Detachment is a clear, if subconscious, attempt not to feel what is really happening, or its significance. It leads to emotional numbness.

Trust is defined as reliance on another.[44]

Trusting the Lord is not optional for the born-again person; it is imperative. Why? He commands it. You are made of dust. He knows you need someone upon whom to rely. He commands you to be strong. You need his indwelling presence through the Holy Spirit in order to be strong.

---

[43] *Merriam-Webster's Collegiate Dictionary*, 11th ed., s.v. "detach."
[44] Ibid., s.v. "trust."

Because of who God is, this is a legitimate command. His faithfulness, strength, wisdom, love, power, and every other attribute—all are perfect in every way. He has provided salvation for people everywhere, though not all have accepted it. If he were not perfect, his provision of salvation would be unfounded. There would be no guarantee of redemption or eternal life. There is, however, a guarantee, because of his faithfulness that cannot be broken. It is not in the nature of God to lie. Satan is the father of lies; Satan has no part in God (John 14:30).

Because of the frailty of your human condition and your enormous vulnerabilities, you will, in all likelihood, try trusting in something or someone.

In a sermon given at Community Presbyterian Church, Ventura, California, on January 5, 2014, the Reverend Kent Meads expressed the human need to belong as a God-given gift ignited when your mother holds you at birth. The need lasts as long as life does. While not interchangeable, I would include in that need to belong the need to be loved. God presents himself as the essence of love, the definition of love, and the ultimate expression of love. As it says, "Greater love has no one than this, that someone lay down his life for his friends" (John 15:13). Jesus did that.

God describes himself as your lover, the father to the fatherless, the sustainer of the widow, the one who is altogether faithful, never forsaking you. He expressed the fulfillment of his love in sending his Son, Jesus, to pay the penalty for your sins. Jesus's death, his resurrection, and his gift of the Holy Spirit are the guarantees of your entrance into heaven if you have put your trust in him and responded to his gift of salvation. He is your Redeemer and Savior, the one who bought you back from Satan's control. He is your Deliverer.

His love is shown in other ways in creating both the universe and nature: the sun, the moon, the stars, the seasons, food, water, and air. All are gifts of love given to you, his child, by a heavenly Father. While God's love is universal, that love does not always filter down to love within and between persons in the human community, even between his own children.

Reality

Sin can result in acts of violence and betrayal between any two or more of his children. Acts of child abuse can be as detrimental within the family of God as they are outside his family, in the general culture. Other forms of sin are often as frequent within the church, also called the body of Christ, as they are outside the church. This is a tragedy. Followers of Christ, who are supposed to be salt and light to the world, are often guilty of the same offenses as unbelievers. The recipients of his great and enormous love often violate his command to love one another as he has loved them. They fail to exercise the empowerment of the Holy Spirit.

God's love is to be demonstrated most intimately by our parents, who are our earliest influences, then by friendships, and later in life by marriage partners.

What is the likely result when those who are charged with giving love most intimately disobey?

Psychology presents many pictures of people who have not been loved by those closest to them. Acting out, anxiety, depression, detachment, drunkenness, murder, and many other wrong behaviors result.

List some of the problems of someone you know who has not been loved.

Personal History

In my clinical practice, I specialized in treating anxiety and depression. These are currently the most frequent diagnoses in our culture. In my own life, anxiety had been a constant companion since I was ten. As I grew older, I attempted to protect myself from the feelings of anxiety by detaching: by separating my emotions from whatever I was experiencing in the real world. I became quite successful at it. In time, I could endure emotional assaults by becoming numb.

One of the most severe emotional injuries occurred in my marriage just before I returned to school to obtain my degrees. My pastor at the time prayed with me frequently and provided enough emotional support that I was able to get through the pain within a year. I began my reentry into the world of academics with joy and enthusiasm. The years of my educational and internship experiences were a delight. I had always enjoyed learning and studying; this was no exception.

During that time, the emotional pain sometimes became intense. My detachment was effective enough to allow me to maintain my grades. As a part of my graduate program, I was required to have a certain number of hours of personal psychotherapy. During the therapy the enormity of my pain started to enter my awareness. I was not yet aware of the magnitude of the detachment.

During the first twenty years of my practice, the detachment had not yet become permanent. I sustained one of the worst emotional wounds of my life just prior to moving to a beautiful place on the central coast. I was unable to work for six months. At the end of the six months, I opened a new office on the central coast of California. You may wonder how I maintained a psychological practice if I were numb: by God's grace. He gave me anointing to practice when I would walk into my office, when I was teaching or speaking publicly, or when I was asked a professional or spiritual question. I could feel it. It would lift when I left at the end of the day or event. God says his grace is sufficient (2 Corinthians 12:9). It truly is.

As mentioned earlier, I had several years of psychotherapy, after which I started dealing with my anxiety from a spiritual perspective. Why God or I had chosen detachment as my defense mechanism rather than some other form, I don't know. Detachment is part of the anxiety spectrum. While detachment is a psychological defense mechanism it can, if practiced enough, become a tool of the enemy, as can any defense mechanism. Psychology has not determined why one chooses one form of defense rather than another. Sometimes a person close to you, who models a particular defense, can influence your choice. The short answer is that whatever works to help you distance yourself from the pain is the one you develop. I am grateful God protected me from some of the more socially harmful defenses, such as drunkenness, violence, and promiscuity. His grace was so abundant in his protection during that time.

As I explored why I had chosen to detach, I became aware, again, that the short answer was the best. I did not trust that God loved me. I had been raised in a Christian home and church, accepted his salvation at age eight, was baptized at age twelve, was educated in a Christian high school, yet I did not know or trust that God loved me. I didn't even know that it is sin not to trust God. I was not aware of the enormity of the sin of not trusting him until later. Subconsciously I was calling God a liar. Not good!

If you don't trust God, in whom do you trust? Who or what is taking the place of God? Take some time to reflect: in whom you have placed your trust instead of God?

How has that worked out for you? It is called idolatry.

Biblical Persons Who Trusted God

It's All about Him referred to the lives of several people in the Old Testament who trusted God in various situations, some of which were very difficult (Brittell 2014, 127–132). Abraham, Moses, and David, are among the most prominent. Peter and Paul stand out in the New Testament. Hebrews 11 refers to many more.

What are your feelings about their situations? How do you think you would have responded in their circumstances?

Several people's trust did waver. However, the Lord brought them through the situations in such a way that their faith was strengthened and God was glorified. Record some of the situations in which your faith either held firm or wavered and how the Lord brought you through them.

Two people whom I discussed in *It's All about Him* are Mary and Joseph, the mother and stepfather of Jesus (Brittell 2014, 133). There is no record of their trust in God wavering. Their circumstances were among the most unusual in all human history.

Could you have done as well?

How have you expressed your trust in him in the most difficult situation(s) you have faced up to this time in your history?

When I asked myself that question, I had to acknowledge I hadn't trusted. I chose detachment instead.

Hope

The ability to trust is based on hope. *Hope* is defined as "to cherish a desire with anticipation."[45] To *cherish* is "to hold dear."[46] Trust and reliance are also part of hope. You hope that God is who he says he is. You hope that all the attributes of God mentioned in Scripture are true. You hope he has a desire to bless you and to bring you through whatever river of stress or of pain you are trying to cross. You hope his love for you is everlasting. You hope every promise he has given in the Bible is true. You hope that those who have come through their own times of stress and found him to be faithful are giving a truthful account of how he was with them and sometimes carried them. Psalm 42:5 says, "Hope in God; for I shall again praise him, my salvation and my God." Again, it is an imperative. God has provided for all your needs and for many of your wants. His faithfulness is the basis for hope.

---

[45] *Merriam-Webster's Collegiate Dictionary*, 11th ed., s.v. "hope."
[46] Ibid., s.v. "cherish."

Record your thoughts and feelings about trusting in God based on your hope that everything he has said is true.

Neither Trusting nor Hoping in God

My own choice to stop trusting God and to detach from psychological pain began in high school. After several years of marriage, I experienced an event that left me choosing to detach more intensely. This period of numbness lasted for years as the event kept being repeated. Then came a real blow to my spirit and soul. I became almost completely numb for a period of several years.

What was and is fascinating to me is that I felt the anointing of God to continue to do psychotherapy during all this time of personal detachment. I had each office dedicated to God as I moved from one part of the state to another. The anointing felt as though it stayed in each office as I left at the end of the day. Of course, I know the anointing was from God, and he released it at the appropriate time, whether in my offices, speaking engagements, teaching events, or times of prayer for others. Many people's lives were changed.

In what defense mechanism have you trusted to help you cope with the pain in your life? What habits have you developed?

Remember Abraham and Hagar? They brought Ishmael into the world because Abraham and Sarah did not trust or hope in God. Only an omnipotent God can redeem situations from our lack of trust and hope.

Record some times when you gave up hope and trust.

Hope Fulfilled

Shortly after another move, my husband's death, gamma knife radiosurgery for a brain tumor, my retirement, and several other stressful events, the Lord led me to a church where God used the pastor to reach through the numbness with his sermons, listening skills, and friendship. Hope was reborn. Over a period of five years, the numbness was reversed. I was able to feel and to experience the love of God and others in my life in a way I had never known.

Being able to love and trust God is a wonderful gift from Him. He initiates the relationship. He gives you the ability to respond positively. *It's All about Him* refers to several passages that caution you against trusting in man (Brittell 2014, 126). An adolescent with whom I was working clinically, challenged me to justify my position that it is not biblical to trust in man. I did an in-depth word study on trust. It became very clear from Scripture that you are to put your trust in God; you are not to trust in man, not even in those with whom you are very close. After the fall in the Garden of Eden, all people are subject to human frailties.

Disappointment with another person's inability to be trustworthy often leads to depression. This may occur in many different life situations. In my case, the violation of our vows led to detachment rather than depression. As mentioned earlier, why a person chooses one defense mechanism rather than another has not been answered by psychology. Only God knows.

What is clear is that using the defense mechanism keeps the pain at bay, at least briefly. As with most things, the more the defense is used, the stronger it becomes. By God's grace, he didn't create you to be defensive. He created you to live and love in victory and grace. What a good God: he is faithful forever. Whatever psychological or spiritual pain you commit to him, he will heal. He will never leave you or forsake you. You can and must trust God in every aspect of your life. He is the only one who can heal every wound. He is the only one who is God. He will love you forever. *Hope in God!*

Record your thoughts. What is your primary defense mechanism? How does it affect your life? From what pain does it protect you?

The Goal

The goal of this chapter was to be self-revealing and personal. It is a truism within psychology that people who are wounded are often drawn to practice in the field in order to heal themselves. The writing of my two books under the titles, *It's All about Him* and *A Path to Restoration* has resulted in a great deal of healing. At some level, I wanted to tell the story of how God can heal the greatest wounds. Over the years, I have been called various things, most of which were not helpful. Among them were "too sensitive" and "brittle" (from my name). It turned out that the sensitivity was very useful in helping me identify the pain in the lives of my patients as well as my own. Galatians 6:3–5 says,

> If anyone thinks he is something, when he is nothing, he deceives himself. But let each one test his own work, and then his reason to boast will be in himself and not in his neighbor. For each will have to bear his own load.

My restoration will be covered more fully in chapter 12. In this chapter, I wanted to explain the significance of my defense mechanism and how effective it can be. I am so grateful the Lord chose the one he did. It protected me from some unbearable pain and allowed me to practice in my chosen, God-directed field. Other areas of my life have been restored along the way. I was able to love God and my neighbor with my mind and strength. Now that my heart and soul are healed, I am able to love God and my neighbor with my heart, soul, mind, and strength, thus fulfilling the Great Commandment—not perfectly but as the goal.

Trust in God

Hope in God

11

CONVICTION, CONSEQUENCES, CONDEMNATION, OR GRACE FROM HIM

**Am I being given grace, being convicted, having
consequences, or being condemned?
I wanted to know.**

Do not be deceived: God is not mocked, for
whatever one sows, that he will also reap.
—Galatians 6:7

Mercy triumphs over judgment.
—James 2:13

Grace

I need to start with grace, since as God's chosen ones, our entire lives
are covered and filled by grace. Vine defines *grace* as "that which bestows
or occasions pleasure, delight, or causes favorable regard."[47] He further

---

[47] *Vine's Concise Dictionary*, s.v. "grace."

stresses the freedom, universality, and spontaneity of grace. "In the case of God's redemptive mercy" toward us and "the pleasure or joy he designs for the recipient," his grace "is set in contrast with debt."[48] Pleasure or joy: what an overwhelming gift! Record your thoughts.

O'Collins and Farrugia speak of "any undeserved gift or help freely and lovingly provided by God, but above all the utterly basic gift of being saved in Christ through faith."[49] Through this grace, you are granted new birth (salvation), the indwelling of the Holy Spirit, adoption as a child of God, and membership in Christ's body. Further, as a result of this grace, you can speak to God in prayer and have him hear and answer your prayers. You can look forward to an eternal home in heaven with him. All the good things mentioned in the preceding ten chapters have been a gift to you. They have come from the hand of God as a result of his grace.

As a graduate student in a PhD psychology program, I was required to study theology. In theology classes, grace was referred to as "unmerited favor." While it is that, merit was not a word I used except in high school with the concept of demerits for unacceptable behavior. As a result, grace became a theological construct sitting on a bookshelf rather than the living breathing grace of God that blesses and supports my entire life and being. I did not fully understand this part of God's love and grace until recently.

How did I miss this most important aspect of the love of God for his children? When I asked my mentor if *undeserved* could be used instead of *unmerited*, it all fell into place. I can understand God's undeserved favor. All his gifts are undeserved. By his grace, it has always been there, whether I understood it or not. Grace is such an overwhelming gift that you, too, may not have understood the fullness of its meaning. Undeserved favor: who among us deserves the favor of God?

---

[48] Ibid.
[49] O'Collins and Farrugia, *Concise Dictionary of Theology*, s.v. "grace."

As you studied in earlier chapters, you learned that you were born dead in sin. You deserve eternal separation from God since he cannot bear to look upon sin. How is it, then, that you can stand before God justified and covered in righteousness? Jesus's death, resurrection, and ascension have given you the covering you need before God. That is called mercy.

Mercy

Mercy is a gift of God's grace. That is why mercy triumphs over judgment.

Mercy is defined by Vine as *"the outward manifestation of pity.* It assumes need on the part of him who receives it, and resources adequate to meet the need on the part of him who shows it.*"*[50] O'Collins and Farrugia define mercy as "God's loving care for all creatures, especially human beings, which invites us in turn to empathize with and alleviate the misery of others."[51] Mercy is another of God's overwhelming gifts.

How does it feel to think of God pitying you? Is your first reaction "I don't need to be pitied; I can get along without pity"? Really? How is that working out for you?

When you think of some of the choices you have made and the painful consequences you have had to live with as a result, can you be grateful for the pity of God? How grateful are you that you didn't have to live with those consequences for the whole of eternity? Record your thoughts.

---

[50] *Vine's Concise Dictionary*, s.v. "mercy," emphasis added.
[51] O'Collins and Farrugia, *Concise Dictionary of Theology*, s.v. "mercy."

A simple cry for help is, in reality, a cry for his mercy and grace. How often do you need help?

How often do you recognize that you need help?

In the opening Scriptures of this chapter, it might seem as though God is contradicting himself. Which is it: will I reap what I sow or will I receive mercy? God is making it clear that both are real options. It is up to him to decide which one he will choose to use and when. He uses both: grace and mercy are part of every interaction with God. Being able to breathe is an act of mercy and grace. Reaping what you sow includes all the blessings that come from your acts of love and obedience to him. Record your reactions.

Conviction

Conviction is one place where you see God using both grace and mercy. *Merriam-Webster's* says that to *convict* is to prove or "convince of error or sinfulness."[52] Outside of a courtroom situation where the outcome has already been decided, conviction usually comes in the form of an uncomfortable feeling or a feeling of *dis*ease. This suggests you are doing something wrong or offending God.

The most important thing to remember about conviction is that it is a gift of his grace, given by God through the Holy Spirit. It is not a ministering gift of the Spirit in the same sense that wisdom and healing are gifts. It is a gift in the sense that when you are doing something wrong, the Lord calls it to your attention through the conviction of the Holy

---

[52] *Merriam-Webster's Collegiate Dictionary*, 11th ed., s.v. "convict."

Spirit. Jesus says, "If I do not go away, the Helper will not come to you. But if I go, I will send him to you. And when he comes, he will convict the world concerning sin and righteousness and judgment" (John 16:7–8). Conviction can help you stop what you are doing that is against God's will and repent. To *repent* is to "turn from sin and dedicate oneself to the amendment of one's life … to feel regret or contrition."[53]

Why does God bother convicting you?

One of the goals of the Father, Son, and Holy Spirit is to bring you to the truth. *Truth* is verifiable, "the body of real things, events, and facts."[54] The Lord does not want you wandering around in confusion, lies, and sin. *It's All about Him* (Brittell 2014, 140–141) gives examples of several occasions of conviction: Pharaoh's household (Genesis 12, 20), Joseph's brothers (Genesis 44:13–16), David (Psalm 51), the Pharisees (Matthew 5:20), and the Pharisees who were trying to condemn the woman taken in adultery (John 8). The book also shows how people responded differently to conviction. Joseph's brothers wept, David repented, and the Pharisees condemned the Lord to death. Even when convicted, people can continue in sin. Jesus used different methods to provide conviction. Sometimes he used confrontation (the Pharisees), and at other times he chided (Martha, Luke 10:40) or used a look (Peter, Luke 22:61).

How old were you when you first became aware of conviction?

Of what have you been convicted?

What did you do with the conviction?

---

[53]   Ibid., 11th ed., s.v. "repent."

[54]   Ibid., s.v. "truth."

If you don't follow conviction to repentance, you are likely to incur consequences.

Consequences

A *consequence* is a conclusion derived through logic.[55] Don't you just love that? You wander around and wonder why or how in the world this happened. If you would apply some logic with prayer, in all likelihood, the answer would become very clear. You would be able to see a relationship between some behavior on your part and what you are experiencing in the moment.

In the natural world, you take for granted that if you plant a carrot seed, you will harvest a carrot—and the same with any other kind of plant. This also applies in the animal kingdom. Mating two of any kind will produce another of the same kind.

Yet in the psychological or spiritual world, people appear amazed when their behavior results in an outcome with similar characteristics. In eating the fruit in the Garden of Eden, Adam and Eve ate something that had reproduction of itself built right in: ultimate death for all living things.

You need to remember that the garden was the original setting for humanity. Reproduction takes place in a garden, sometimes without your awareness. Seeds fall to the ground, God provides the growth system, and amazingly you have a plant just like the original, *carrying its reproductive system within its own seed.* The same applies to the animal kingdom. This principle is important. Your behavior is carrying the potential for reproduction right within itself. God said you will reap what you sow. The plan for reproduction, and therefore for consequences, is held within the original behavior. This applies to the good reaping as well as the painful.

Have you assumed that your behavior has no consequences and that the universe is random, that there is no relationship between cause

---

[55]   *Merriam-Webster's Collegiate Dictionary,* 11th ed., s.v. "consequence."

and effect? God says clearly that there is a relationship, either negative or positive.

People often confuse consequences with lack of forgiveness or punishment. In my office, the question often came up. "I asked both God and the person whom I had hurt to forgive me. Why am I still suffering the consequences?" If you look at those who preceded us, you find that consequences can last for millennia. You still read about the failures and sins of some of the most outstanding heroes of the faith, such as David and Moses. They obviously were forgiven long ago. But the awareness of their sins lingers through time. That is part of the consequence as well as a part of God's grace.

Scripture says God forgives and forgets our sin. *Forgiveness* means to give up resentment or to give up relief from payment.[56] It releases a person from the burden of guilt; you no longer hold the issue against them. You no longer resent them. When God forgives you, he no longer holds your sin against you. He forgets the sin in terms of judgment or punishment. But the consequence is still in effect.

For example, you may have broken your arm. Perhaps the arm has been healed and restored to full use. However, you will never have that arm as though it was never broken. The scars of the surgery necessary to repair it may be visible for a lifetime. You may have rods or screws or plates in place to hold it for the rest of your life. You may have stopped being angry about what caused the incident. However, the memory may be there until eternity.

In *It's All about Him*, I listed several possible events that might occur to you in thinking about the life of Peter (Brittell 2014, 143). Each event was a consequence of prior, knowable facts. He was forgiven for all those that were sin. However, you still remember them. Only God forgets, for the purpose of judgment. He is the only who has the right to pass judgment.

How do you understand forgiveness?

---

[56]   *Merriam-Webster's Collegiate Dictionary*, 11th ed., s.v. "forgiveness."

Have you repented and asked for forgiveness for some sin you have committed? Have you felt the grace of his forgiveness?

Do you find it interesting that there is no record of Adam and Eve ever repenting of their sin? Repentance was not a part of the relationship with God until after the Israelites had been called out as a chosen people and the Ten Commandments were given (Exodus 20). The Bible refers to the law as being the teacher. God gave the law to help you recognize what sin is: to make you aware of the things that offend him. In the Old Testament, animal sacrifices represented conviction and consequences.

In the New Testament, Paul suffered some really difficult events. When you remember that he also persecuted Christians with some of the same tortures that he experienced, you see the connection. In God's economy, it is logical that Paul would have to reap what he sowed. However, he was given grace and mercy to endure the severe consequences he experienced. He also harvested the godly things he had done and was able to live an abundant and contented life.

How have you experienced consequences that you could relate to causal behavior?

What did you do with the consequences?

Then, there is the Christ. He suffered all the consequences for all the sins that have ever been committed. When you think of just your own sin for just one day and multiply that by the trillions of sins committed by all of us throughout history, it is no wonder Christ asked his Father if it would be possible for this cup to pass from him. I, personally, cannot fully fathom his sacrifice for me. I can meditate on it, but even then, it is beyond my comprehension: that kind of love and his willingness to carry the punishment for all that sin. Praise and thanksgiving, and giving him control of my life so that he can live again in human form through me, are the only things I can offer in return.

How have you praised him for consequences?

In nature you clearly see the relationship between sowing and reaping: you expect to harvest what you planted. What you eat will show up in your clothing size and your health. Somehow, people don't seem to carry that same expectation over into the psychological or spiritual realms. However, God does. Your reaping can result in positive rewards or in negative consequences in the behavioral realm. Your spiritual commitment will be obvious in your spiritual choices. You cannot hide from God. Your reward (reaping) exposes the nature of your choices.

Condemnation

To *condemn* is to declare to be wrong or evil, unfit for use.[57] Jesus was condemned for each one of us and for all of us. In an earlier chapter, I explained that he was declared evil in your place while you were declared righteous in his place. This is an exchange made by his blood. What an incredible exchange! This is the most significant exchange made in the history of the world.

It's All about Him gives several examples of both people and situations in which God considered condemnation appropriate (Brittell 2014, 145). Then it presents several passages declaring that you, who are chosen by God to be adopted into his family, are not condemned. What a supreme free gift. While you, as his child, will experience consequences—both punishments and blessings—you are not condemned. You are not considered unfit for use!

How can you not be overwhelmed by his grace and mercy?

---

[57] *Merriam-Webster's Collegiate Dictionary*, 11th ed., s.v. "condemn."

Condemnation, as a rule, brings with it punishment. The Christ was punished for your, my, and everyone's sin by death on a cross. Jesus bore the condemnation from God the Father for the sins of the whole world—*everyone* throughout history.

If that gets your attention, how do you respond?

God is the one who ultimately decides which of the four—conviction, consequences, condemnation, or mercy—will be the appropriate course of action. Judas experienced conviction, consequences, and condemnation, all but mercy. Peter, on the other hand, experienced conviction, consequences, and mercy but not condemnation. Examine your own life. If you are born again, Jesus has already paid your condemnation even though you may have experienced conviction, consequences, and certainly mercy.

What new thoughts have come to your awareness?

How do you see grace and mercy differently from how you did?

The Goal

The goal of this chapter is to help you become aware of the Holy Spirit's function in terms of conviction. He convicts you of sin. He also helps you recognize consequences if you don't stop sinning and repent at that point. The natural process of consequences is not changed just because the issue might be psychological or spiritual in nature. Those who do not stop sinning when they are convicted will most likely experience consequences and may, ultimately, incur condemnation.

Overarching all of the above is mercy: God's choice to feel pity for you and to provide for you what you could never provide for yourself. He remembers that you are made of dust. He remembers that the enemy of your soul is the same enemy who tried to get Jesus to worship him during his period of temptation (Luke 4).

God's grace is the ultimate gift he could have given you. It is manifest every day in the air he gives you to breathe and the ability he gives you to breathe it. He has made it possible for you to be adopted into his family. He has given his children eternal life with himself: children with their Father. He has given a beautiful universe in which to run, play, and explore. He has met every need and many wants. *He has given you his love.*

In Christ, there is no condemnation.

12

Restoration by Him

**I have been restored.
I wanted you to know.**

He restores my soul.
—Psalm 23:5

To *restore* is "to put or bring back into existence or use ... or put back into a former or original state."[58]

Restoration, like all God's gifts, is an act of his amazing grace. God is the only one in the universe to have the wisdom, power, and love to accomplish restoration. That is because he is the only one who is sovereign.

Sovereignty means "supreme excellence ... supreme power ... freedom from external control."[59] That describes God. Everything you have seen, heard, touched, tasted, experienced, or felt began with the sovereign, perfect, holy God.

How amazing is that, when you let yourself think about it?

---

[58]   *Merriam-Webster's Collegiate Dictionary*, 11th ed., s.v. "restore."
[59]   Ibid., 11th ed., s.v. "sovereignty."

David describes God's sovereignty well in 1 Chronicles 29, the verses with which I began this book. David experienced God intimately in almost every aspect of his life.

The sovereign Lord does things that are very personal: he gives me an instructed tongue to know what to say to the weary. He awakens my ear to hear his voice (Isaiah 50:4). These gifts were invaluable to me in the practice of clinical psychology and in the whole of my life. Recognizing the voice of the Holy Spirit is a necessary gift for every Christian. He vindicates me, according to Isaiah 50. Isaiah knew God well. Jesus's disciples had the privilege of living and working with him personally for three years. That is an enormous gift. After that, they lived and worked with him through the power of the Holy Spirit. You, too, can live and work with him through the power of the Holy Spirit in your life.

Restoration

You can be restored when you surrender your life to him. God's power to restore ultimately reverses the fall that took place in the Garden of Eden. From being consigned to separation from God—being cast out of the garden—you can be restored to full relationship with him on this earth and enjoy eternal life with him. This is an equally enormous gift for you. In *It's All about Him*, I listed several people who were restored from various conditions, including death (Brittell 2014, 153).

During the course of my graduate work, I became aware of St. Francis, of whom it was said that he could hear the voice of God more clearly than he heard the voice of the man standing next to him. My soul craved that kind of intimacy. I set aside a day and a chair once a week for the sole purpose of learning to recognize the voice of the Holy Spirit. It took a great deal of practice. I would be distracted so easily. I would wait, pray, read the Bible, meditate, and pray some more. After spending one day a week for a year, in prayer, study, and meditation on God, I could hear the voice of the Holy Spirit clearly. I am still guided by hearing his voice. It takes continual communication (speaking and waiting) to hear from him. David speaks of waiting on God. David was a man after God's own heart.

Do you want less for yourself?

In today's culture, numerous TV shows are based on the restoration of old, dilapidated, or ruined houses. I wanted to be an interior designer when I returned to college after having raised children. Having the heart of a designer, I am always fascinated by the final outcome: how something tawdry can be turned into something beautiful. When I prayed about becoming an interior designer, the Lord said he wanted me to restore the inside of people, not their houses. I became a psychologist and worked for several decades in that field. I loved the work, and the Lord blessed it.

In *It's All about Him*, I stated that my restoration took three and a half years (Brittell, 2014, 159). I thought the restoration was complete at that time. How wrong I was. It took more than five years and is continuing to this day. It took several decades for me to become an emotionally broken, numb person. My pastor's ministry was the human means the Lord used to bring about my restoration.

What broke me? A few weeks before his death, my husband of several decades told me why he had never loved me. He felt his inability to love me was the result of never having learned to love. His confession was the straw that, in this case, broke my heart. The pain that had been buried in my subconscious through detachment came to the surface and into my awareness over the five years of my restoration. Given that detachment was my defense mechanism, and that detachment leads to numbness, I had chosen, subconsciously, to become almost totally numb. Emotions of almost any kind were numb. Joy, sadness—I couldn't feel any of them except in very small doses.

It took more than five years for me to be restored to being a person who was able to feel almost everything. Periods of felt emotion occurred occasionally during that five-year period, but they were short-lived. It was Good Friday of 2015 when I finally accepted God's forgiveness personally. Second Corinthians 6:14 says not to be unequally yoked to an unbeliever in marriage. That sin led to decades of pain and numbness. It originated because I did not trust God.

A line from the sermon delivered by my pastor finally broke through. He said, "You are not that person anymore." That is what Christ does for us. He makes us new creatures. He restores us.

It took over five years for emotional stability to be restored. Detachment had begun when I was six. It took many years to develop into total numbness. I am again able to love God and my neighbor with my heart. Since the soul is considered the organizing principle of the human being, I am able to love God and my neighbor with my soul as well. Loving God and my neighbor is the essence of life. It is the greatest commandment. God is love. Writing this book and the original *It's All about Him* have been very helpful in restoring the parts of my soul that I thought were numb forever.

Rejection is a powerful influence. The Bible, particularly the Old Testament, is full of accounts of God's pain and anger at being rejected by his chosen people. He pleaded, threatened, and finally sent them into exile because they refused to return his love for them. He is God. Yet he felt their rejection keenly. I am made in his image. Why was I surprised that I would feel rejection just as keenly, allowing for the differences between being divine and being human?

Some things God has restored for me are the following:

- dignity
- emotional stability
- health
- joy
- respect
- the ability to feel
- the ability to love

What has broken your heart?

What has God restored in your life that makes clear his love for you? Write the story of your own restoration.

The Goal

The goal of this chapter has been to help you see that restoration is possible. "With God, all things are possible" (Matthew 19:26). No matter how grievous the pain or the sin, Jesus was born, died, and was resurrected to pay for that sin and to restore you to full faith and functioning. He came that you might have an abundant life (John 10:10). I invite you to ask Him to restore you to the abundant life. The greatest restoration of all time took place when Jesus was restored to his throne in heaven (Philippians 2). He grants us the grace to participate in his restoration. If you have not yet been restored, ask God for restoration.

David says, "He restores my soul" (Psalm 23).
I agree with him.

He has restored my soul.

SOURCES

Brittell, Lois. *It's All about Him: Intimacy with God.* Bloomington, IN: WestBow Press, 2014.

Douthat, Ross. *Bad Religion: How We Became a Nation of Heretics.* New York: Free Press, 2012.

Guralnik, D. B. (ed.). *Webster's New World Dictionary.* New York: Simon & Schuster, 1986.

Hudson, Hugh; David Puttnam; Colin Welland; Nicholas Farrell; Nigel Havers; Ian Charleson; Ben Cross, et al, 2005. *Chariots of Fire.* Burbank, CA: Warner Home Video.

Brother Lawrence, *The Practice of the Presence of God.* Springdale, PA: Whitaker House, 1982.

Meads, Kent. *Belonging.* Sermon. Ventura, CA: Community Presbyterian Church, January 5, 2014.

Mish, Frederick C. (ed.) *Merriam-Webster's Collegiate Dictionary.* 11th ed. Springfield, MA: Merriam-Webster, Inc., 2012.

O'Collins, G. S., and E. G Farrugia. *A Concise Dictionary of Theology.* New York: Paulist Press, 2000.

VanderGriend, A. J. *Discover Your Gifts: and Learn How to Use Them.* Grand Rapids, MI: CRC Publications, 1996.

Vine, W. E. *Vine's Concise Dictionary of the Bible.* Nashville: Thomas Nelson, 2005.

AFTERWORD

After publishing my original book, *It's All about Him: Intimacy with God* (Brittell, 2014), I received inquires from readers why I had not provided room for note taking and answering questions. Making notes seems to imprint ideas more effectively than reading alone. That was the reason for the birth of this book. As in the original book, I used as few outside sources as possible.

In writing the second book, I found greater intimacy with God than I had experienced writing the first book. I understood forgiveness in a more personal way, not as a theological construct but as his having *forgiven* me and *restored* me to the intimacy I had with him as a teenager. There was more freedom and joy in understanding the relevant scriptures. It gave me a hunger for even greater intimacy with the Savior and Restorer of my soul.

I wish that same response for you as you read it. I pray that God grants you a greater hunger for intimacy with him and a greater understanding of what he has done for you, of how much he loves you, and that peace with God is available to you. I pray that you enjoy his Word in a brand-new way. I pray that those who read this book find faith, hope, love, forgiveness, peace, intimacy with God, and restoration.

Again, I wish to thank my pastor, Rev. Kent Meads, for his friendship and ministry in my life. God chose him to be the instrument of restoration. I also wish to thank Rev. Wayne Kempton for his encouragement, support and editorial work. Without their faithfulness to what God called them to be and do, this book would not have been written.

Today, if you hear his voice, do not harden your hearts.
—Hebrews 3:7, 15; 4:7

Let us therefore strive to enter that rest, so that no one may fall by the same sort of disobedience. For the word of the Lord is living and active, sharper than any two-edged sword, piercing to the division of soul and spirit, of joints and marrow, and discerning the thoughts and intentions of the heart.
—Hebrews 4:11–12

I will take joy in the God of my salvation. God, the Lord is my strength.
---Habakkuk 3:18b—19a

Thank you Jesus
Lois Brittell, 2016

IT ALWAYS WILL BE ALL ABOUT HIM

Printed in the United States
By Bookmasters